ASIA MYSTERIOSA

ZAM BHOTIVA

ASIA MYSTERIOSA

L'Oracle de Force Astrale
comme moyen de communication avec
« Les Petites Lumières d'Orient »

PRÉCÉDÉ D'UNE PRÉFACE DE F. DIVOIRE
ET D'ÉTUDES PAR MAURICE MAGRE ET J. MARQUÈS-RIVIÈRE

DORBON-AÎNÉ
19, Boulevard Haussmann, 19
PARIS

Asia Mysteriosa

(ASIA THE MYSTERIOUS)

The Oracle of Astral Force
as a means of communication with
'The Little Lights of the East'

PRECEDED BY A PREFACE BY
FERNAND DIVOIRE
AND ESSAYS BY MAURICE MAGRE AND
JEAN MARQUÈS-RIVIÈRE

First English Translation

Polair
Publishing

POLAIR PUBLISHING · LONDON

Original publication in French, 1929
First English translation October 2012

British Library Cataloguing in Publication Data
A catalogue record for this book is available
from the British Library

ISBN 978-1-905398-27-0

*Set in 11.5 on 14 & 12.5 on 15.5 pt Bodoni Book by the
Publisher and printed and bound by Halstan Printing Group,
Amersham, Buckinghamshire HP6 6HJ*

CONTENTS

PUBLISHERS' NOTE

In reproducing *Asia Mysteriosa*, although this is a translation and not a facsimile, we have tried to be as faithful to the visible appearance of the original as we can. For instance, we have put numerals in figures throughout to match the original and acknowledge the numerology which underscores the work. We have, however, slightly reduced the number of capital letters used and have modernised some spellings to give modern English forms for proper names. Numbered footnotes are from the French text; footnotes identified by asterisks and daggers and in sans-serif type are editorial comments new to this edition.

Italics are used for the actual answers of the Oracle, for the title *Asia Mysteriosa* and for the *Bulletin* of the Polaires.

The latest correspondence of Zam Bhotiva (Cesare Accomani) that the editor has seen is from 1956 and he is believed to have died late in that decade. Mario Fille, his collaborator, died earlier. We have made all proper enquiries about the copyright position of this work, and have acknowledged the estate of the author as the copyright-holder.

In preparing a text we are grateful to the archive of the White Eagle Lodge and Publishing Trust for providing working copies of both *Asia Mysteriosa* and the Polaire *Bulletins*, and to the Publishing Trust for permitting quotation from White Eagle books. Finally, we should like to thank the translator, M.P., who wishes her work to remain anonymous beyond her initials, and those who have read the manuscript for comment, proofing and correction: Ian Sumter, Dave Patrick and, most of all, Nigel Millross.

Asia Mysteriosa, and the Polaires

COLUM HAYWARD

Asia Mysteriosa presents to the world an oracle that apparently produces life-changing answers by arithmetical calculations derived simply from the phrasing of a question. It was first published in 1929 and written by an author using the pen-name Zam Bhotiva, but with many acknowledgments to others in the footnotes and elsewhere. It carried, as it does here, no less than three prefaces commending it. The following year, the first issue appeared of a monthly journal entitled *Le Bulletin des Polaires*, 'the Polaire Bulletin'. As the name implies, it was the mouthpiece of a group who were known as 'the Polaires', and the core of this group had worked quietly with the Oracle for much of the preceding decade. Their own formation into a larger, defined group is described by the author of *Asia Mysteriosa* in an Appendix (below, p. 155). My words here are therefore not only to introduce an extraordinary phenomenon from the world of esotericism, but also to shed light on seekers who might otherwise remain in the shadows, although many of them were quite conspicuous names in pre-War Paris.

Most of us today associate oracles with the Greco-Roman world, and our minds run primarily to the one at Delphi, so to find that an oracle made a new appearance in the twentieth century, or that it should be offered to the public in English in the twenty-first, may somewhat shake our understanding of what is current in modern life. It can scarcely have been less of a surprise to see it at the end of the 1920s. Yet it seems to have been remarkably well received by at least a slice of the Paris intelligentsia, since (after seeing the Oracle in action) no less than four of them wrote prefatory material for the book. They were a newspaper editor, Fernand Divoire; a colourful man of letters, Maurice Magre (noted novelist, playwright, opium-taker and student of the Cathars or Albigenses); Jean Marquès-Rivière, author of authoritative works on Tibetan mysticism; and, the biggest name of all, co-founder of the Traditionalist school in anthropology, René Guénon. Guénon's preface did not make it to publication, because of a row with the sponsors of the Oracle that was never healed.* He had corrected the text of the book, seen the proof, and seems even to have allowed his footnotes to be used.

So how did the twentieth century come to discover such an unlikely source of curiosity, even wisdom? The story is quite fairytale, and indeed it was written up as such in a popular paperback of 1934. I will here summarise it in four simple scenes, using the short account in *Asia Mysteriosa*, a much fuller one in the Polaire *Bulletin* in 1930, René Thimmy's LA MAGIE À PARIS (Paris, 1934, the 'fairytale' story),† and P. Geyraud's LES SOCIÉTÉS SECRÈTES DE PARIS (Paris, 1938), which takes much detail from Thimmy.

Scene I is the village of Bagnaia, outside Viterbo, which in turn is just beyond the northern rim of the 'seven hills' that circle Rome. The year is 1908, and a father is here visiting, with his son, for the holidays. The boy is still quite young; his father is French, but lives in Rome. As a holiday destination Bagnaia has just one attraction: the sixteenth-century Mannerist garden of the Villa Lante. It is accessible by train, and that is about all we know about how or why they are there, seventy miles from home.#

Almost at once, the boy's attention 'was drawn to an old man wearing the coarse monkish habit. Tall, ascetic, sunburnt, his eyes deep set, he passed along the streets as though in a dream.

*The Polaire *Bulletin* of 9 March 1931 prints this preface in full. See p. 19.
†See below, p 13.
#Details of the visit are from the Polaire *Bulletin*, 9 June 1930.

'The lad made enquiries from the country folk. Was this man a godly hermit? No. After listening to what was said, he gathered that this individual, who was called Father Julian, was considered by the dwellers in this little town as one who could cast magical spells—a sorcerer. Although nothing definite in the way of accusation could be brought against him the "presumptions" seemed grave—it would be as well, they said, to beware of this strange person, who lived as a wild man of the woods in an old ruined hut and fed on herbs and fruits; who was scorned by all good Christians and was, moreover, one who had never been seen to cross the threshold of the House of God.…

'In spite of these tales of magical charms and evil spells the young man was greatly drawn to the recluse, by a strange sympathy, and one day he decided to visit him in his hut. He was received as one who had been expected for a long time.'*

A strange friendship develops, with almost daily visits and growing understanding between the two of them. Scene III seems to clinch that association. 'One day on going up the path to the hermit's dwelling, he found Father Julian lying unconscious on the road, badly wounded in the knee. He dressed the deep wound as well as he was able, and then assisted the old man to re-enter his hut. The next day he found the hermit up and about; three days later the wound was completely healed.

'What mysterious herbs had been the means of obtaining this complete restoration to health? The young man did not dare to inquire. Many a time the recluse, when questioned somewhat indiscreetly by his young friend, would remain silent, lost in a dream, the reflection of which shone through his large, dark, far-seeing eyes.'†

We must see this as a defining point in the relationship: later, Thimmy is particularly eloquent about the level of the boy's care: he says that he showed 'a generosity, a sensitivity rarely

---

*Polaire *Bulletin*, 9 June 1930, quoted in English from the translation given in Ivan Cooke's THY KINGDOM COME (London: Wright & Brown, 1933), revised and reprinted as ARTHUR CONAN DOYLE'S BOOK OF THE BEYOND (Liss, 2006). †From the same source.

found among young people'.* From this point the visits become
more frequent, and 'the conversations between them of greater
length and of a more intimate nature. The old man spoke mean-
ingfully of pain and sacrifice to the younger man whose eyes
were still fixed on the dreams and illusions of life.' Pain and
sacrifice are not going to be irrelevant to a story which will
climax with the Second World War, although that dimension is
outside the reach of this Preface. Touchingly, though, the story
of the special caring comes back to us in *Asia Mysteriosa*,
where a dream the boy had many years later is referred to: 'It
was during this dream – the only one in which the operator
saw Father Julian – that the latter showed our friend his knee,
wound round with a yellow handkerchief, saying to him: "I remember…"' 'The operator' is of course the boy.

Scene IV is the moment of separation. 'With a saddened
heart the youth made his way for the last time to the hermit's
abode. It will never be known what the recluse murmured "from
mouth to ear" to him whom he called for the first time his "son".
We can only say that at the moment of leave-taking, he handed
to him some leaves of paper yellowed by the passage of time.
These were "a small fragment from the Book of the Science of
Life and of Death".

'The recipient of these mysterious pages will remember to
the end of his days the last words spoken to him by the Sage:
"Should you at any time require help or counsel you have only
to follow the instructions which are contained in this old manuscript—you will receive your reply. It may even occur that one
day I myself will reply to you. But remember never to divulge
to anyone in the world what is written on these pages, for in so
doing you run the risk for yourself, as well as for the one who
obtains the knowledge, of madness or death."†

Asia Mysteriosa is about those pages. They were, by any
standards, an extraordinary gift to make to a young boy.

*LA MAGIE À PARIS, p. 162, in my own translation. †*Bulletin*, June 1930.

*

My own connection with the printed book, *Asia Mysteriosa*, goes back to when I was a boy too, for I was brought up at New Lands, the Hampshire centre of the White Eagle Lodge, founded in 1936 by my grandmother, Grace Cooke. Because of a connection between the Polaires and White Eagle Lodge, *Asia Mysteriosa* was in the archive, which also contained many Polaire *Bulletins*. Including some photocopies I later received from a contact, we have the *Bulletin* complete from its first issue on 9 May 1930 through to the first one of 1934. My father compiled a short and unpublished history of the Polaires for the archive, based on such limited information as he had, despite careful research such as asking a White Eagle Lodge member based in Paris to make enquiries in bookshops and elsewhere. Later, the archives would become my own province. I have always loved the clear, bold cover designs of the early *Bulletins*.

Today, as the Lodge's Minister and meditation teacher (which may be more relevant than it sounds) at its London premises off Kensington High Street and after a substantial amount of reflection and study, I feel able to give *Asia Mysteriosa* better sympathetic attention than it has typically had. I believe that the connection my grandmother made with the Polaires was a very deep and important one, and I have written about it both in ARTHUR CONAN DOYLE'S BOOK OF THE BEYOND (1994, 2003, 2006) and in an essay in THE VIEW (2009; pp. 44–58). My contributions to each of these books describe visits I have made to Bagnaia and the impression the visits made upon me; I have also visited the Polaires' premises at Avenue Junot, a short walk from the church of the Sacré Coeur in Paris. More importantly, the White Eagle Lodge owes a great deal to the distinctive spirituality of the Polaires, much of which has been obscured by their later divergence into a very different sort of group from the one they formed at the outset. I may cause surprise even with the word 'spirituality', but it is deliberate.

Publication of the first English translation of *Asia Mysteriosa* gives me just a brief opportunity to acknowledge that debt. Although my grandmother, Grace Cooke, and the whole White Eagle brotherhood made a complete break with the Polaires in 1935, in many ways they both defended most of the ideals those early Polaires held as dear. I may be able to speak from the benefit of being around her memories in my own childhood, although she did not speak at length about them. There is an indication of the depth of connection between the Polaires and the White Eagle Lodge in the book ARTHUR CONAN DOYLE'S BOOK OF THE BEYOND, which describes the work they accomplished together: it has been continuously in print under three different titles since 1934. It should be consulted by any interested student as it gives an amount of additional information on the Polaires and on their leaders beyond what it is possible to give here. As far as possible I have tried to use contemporary sources in this edition, believing we have much more to gain from them than from more recent theorising and sensational journalism.

The White Eagle Lodge is a form of Mystery or Wisdom School. In the Mystery Schools, truths were enacted in rituals, covered in layers of myth, even wrapped in disguise. In short, things are not always quite what they seem. When I re-read *Asia Mysteriosa* some forty years on from the first time I looked it over, I began to see it in a new light. Close study pays off. I have come to regard it as a careful teaching manual, although it does not initially come across as such. The reader will have to deal with that statement just as I put it, for I want to prompt some deeper reflection.

*

Let us return to the story of the Oracle. I have spelt it out because, although the encounter at Bagnaia is described so fully in the second **Bulletin**, the details given in *Asia Mysteriosa* itself are slight. Maybe the author, Bhotiva, wanted our concentration on his text. Who was the boy? His first name was Mario – the accounts agree on that – and his second name appears to have been Fille. We know that his father was French, and 'Fille' means 'daughter', but it is a highly unusual surname. Since Mario always seems to have kept himself in the background, not the foreground, it is quite possible that it was not his real name, and it is worth remembering that he came to fame as the keeper of a number of 'feuilles', leaves or folios, or possibly 'feuillets', pages, the word used for them in the June 1930 *Bulletin*. Listening to the vowel may give a valuable clue as to how 'Fille' arose.

For the next chapter of the story it will be good to listen to the affectionate and maybe sceptical style of René Thimmy, who was actually the French writer Maurice Magre, mentioned already as the contributor of a Preface to *Asia Mysteriosa*. Magre is deeply disingenuous in that he writes from firsthand experience but refers to himself in the third person in his account. His book, LA MAGIE À PARIS, rightly puzzled his biographer, Jacques Bédu, because it is so difficult to gauge its tone.* What we do know from Magre's Preface is that he actually found real richness in apparent fairytales: 'One must dream beautiful stories if life is to become beautiful'.† When as Thimmy he refers to the story of Mario and makes of it a fairy tale, we must either see the irony or understand an artful concealment of real belief. Five years separates the two pieces of writing, and the second is deeply sceptical beside the first. Is it playful, does it represent a change of heart, or is it that the difficult political circumstances of the 1930s, of which more later, required disinformation to be put out? Lastly, though, it may simply have been a starving writer writing sensational stories for cash.

How Thimmy continues the story is however delightful. 'F......' is of course Mario Fille, while 'A......' stands for Cesare Accomani, Zam Bhotiva's real name. Mario has just had his gift of the manuscript from Father Julian.

'The young man, without curiosity, threw the manuscript into the bottom of a suitcase, thought no more about it, and continued his life.

*Jacques Bédu, LE LOTUS PERDU. Cahors, 1997.   †Below, p. 41.

'Ten years passed. Then chance led the doggedly common-sensical F...... to Egypt, where he met a fellow countryman, as unlike him as Don Quixote was to Sancho [Panza].

'A...... (or rather, to use the pseudonym he chose himself, Zam Bhotiva) was more grown-up ["un grand garçon"], and had tried various trades, but he thirsted for the supernatural and was haunted by the taste of the wonderful.

'F...... having told him his adventure, long after leaving Father Julian, Zam Bhotiva jumped up.

'What a godsend for a lover of the wonderful!

'As soon as he could he interrogated his comrade about the precious manuscript.

'F...... didn't even remember if he still had it. How could a magical book full of mathematical formulas matter to him?

'Finally, he remembered where it was and pulled it from under a pile of laundry.'

Our information about when the 'feuillets' from the Book of Life, 'full of mathematical formulas' were used is confusing. The June 1930 *Bulletin* says clearly that just two years after the episode at Bagnaia the boy, 'l'âme torturée par la douleur', used it and it brought him exactly the solace he needed. I think 'deux', for two, may be a transcription error for 'dix' or 'douze' (ten or twelve). Geyraud, by contrast, says that 'for years' Mario 'avoided thinking about this strange puzzle' but then links his rediscovery of it to 'great personal suffering'. After following the hermit's instructions to the letter and asking his desperate question, 'he set out on his paper a surprisingly precise reply, illuminated with ineffable kindness and the highest spirituality'. Thimmy, in the quotation, ignores the suffering and gives an interval of ten years. The June 1930 *Bulletin* says that Father Julian's present location was sought through the medium of the manuscript and its instructions in 1918. I am inclined to marry the story of personal distress with the visit to Egypt, at the end of the First World War, as distress accords with the hermit's words and what *Asia Mysteriosa* tells us about the sort of questions this Oracle, as we must now call it, dealt best with. Our 'fairy story' now has a mathematical oracle, and three characters: Fille, his older friend Accomani/Bhotiva, and Father Julian.

We know surprisingly little about Bhotiva. The visit to Egypt upon which he met Mario was an archaeological expedition, and he clearly had much interest in ancient civilization. Already using his maybe Persian *nom-de-plume*, he had written a book as early as 1909 entitled DU MAGNÉTISME PERSONNEL, DE LA CULTURE HUMAINE, with a preface by Ernest Bosc (1837–1913), the author of a dictionary of orientalism, occultism and psychology and at least nine other works.* He clearly had a talent for getting to know people, and people of influence to boot, as the four prefaces to *Asia Mysteriosa* further demonstrate. Three years after *Asia Mysteriosa*, he produced LA MAGIE DANS L'ART DU CHANT and dedicated it to Maurice Magre 'en signe d'affectueuse reconnaissance' – 'with affectionate thanks'. The first book leads us to assume he was born before 1890, but we have little other outward information; we shall return to Bhotiva the man later.

Who, then, was the mysterious Father Julian? *Asia Mysteriosa* tells us little more about him as an Italian than his alternative lifestyle and his name, which of course was 'Padre Giuliano' to the locals. We are told that he 'assuredly wore the sign of the Rose and the Cross' under his outer clothing, and that he disappeared from the village in the year following the meeting, 1909. It mentions the enquiry in 1918, through the Oracle, establishing that he had gone back to the monastery ('couvent') in the Himalaya whence he had come, a period of expiation or atonement over. We discover plenty about his Himalayan life through the Oracle's own replies in *Asia Mysteriosa*, which soon identifies him as as one of three 'Petites Lumières de l'Orient', the Little Lights of the East, of whom more later.

*See http://www.scribd.com/doc/57265963/Esoterisme-Ernest-Bosc-FR-Dictionnaire-de-la-science-occulte-vol2sur2 (consulted 6 Aug. 2012).

There is discussion both in *Asia Mysteriosa* and in Guénon's Preface as to how he could be both 'Padre Giuliano' and a Tibetan wise man, something we cannot fully resolve here.* We know from the Bulletins that a year after the release of *Asia Mysteriosa*, the Lord Buddha 'opened to him the Path of Light' ('La "Voie Lumineuse"' – *Bulletin* of 9 June 1930).

And what about the Oracle itself? It has its own name: L'Oracle de Force Astrale (the Oracle of Astral Force, or Power). *Asia Mysteriosa* tells us almost everything we know about it, and any other reference is derived from its answers, apart from a little bit more in the Polaire *Bulletin*, where a correspondence developed about cabalistic oracles. René Odin, a later 'Chief' of the Polaires, seems to have had a particular interest in these. But *Asia Mysteriosa* (p. 67 and note) denies categorically that the Oracle of Astral Force is Cabalistic.

It is constantly stressed how complicated the calculations were. Maybe for this reason, the Oracle did not like to have its time wasted. Lest that phrase seem flippant, perhaps I should say that the mysterious beings who communicated through the Oracle imposed something of a discipline on their questioners. We shall see how this affected René Guénon (see below, pp. 28, 141–2). Neither, however, did Mario, its operator, like to spend more time on people's questions than he felt he had to. The early Polaire *Bulletin* tells us that he was 'firmly attached … to the things of the world', 'solidement attaché aux choses de la vie'.† It was also hard work for him. A rather amusing exchange occurs in Thimmy's account:

"We are in possession of a special secret, a wonderful cabalistic method, straight from Aladdin's lamp,' exclaimed Zam Bhotiva, as enthusiastic as Don Quixote.

---

*A number of attempts have been made to identify Father Julian; in 1994, Gérard Galtier ventured the suggestion that he was the Italian esotericist Giuliano Kremmerz (EGYPTIAN MASONRY, ROSICRUCIANS AND NEO-CHIVALRY: THE SON OF CAGLIOSTRO, Paris 1994) but the identification is not generally accepted.   †*Bulletin*, 9 June 1930.

'Yes, but…', responded F……-Sancho, who had to spend hours calculating and turning letters into numbers, adding, subtracting, dividing. 'What about me…?'

'We are bringing a beautiful secret to humanity, returned Zam Bhotiva–Don Quixote.'

Asia Mysteriosa not only tells us that a certain section, the 'Preface of Tek the Wise' represented sixty hours of work (p. 62), but it also reminds us that the Delphic Oracle needed to have questions posed to it the night before it responded (p. 122). We are meant to infer that the Oracle of Astral Force also required much of the night to be spent in study before the answer came out.

Although it constantly emphasises numerological connection and number symbolism, one thing *Asia Mysteriosa* does not do for us is to tell us how the Oracle is used, beyond some broad indications set out on pp. 69–70. How could it, when to do so 'involved madness or even death'? However, the Polaires may have struggled with communicating enough of the secret to whet the appetite of readers. Recent French editions have reprinted a further work, A CABALISTIC ORACLE, notionally by Fille and Odin, which does not seem to have been published at the time, but much later, despite an example of a question asked of the Oracle within it bearing a 1935 date. It is a workable oracle, but despite Fille's name being on the cover, it does not fit what we know of his character to suggest he wrote it. Polaire *Bulletins* show that Odin, by contrast, had a particular interest in the subject.*

We can assume that Fille and Bhotiva asked the Oracle of Astral Force some fairly penetrating questions, not least about itself and the communicators who spoke through it. I have de-

*UN ORACLE KABBALISTIQUE was published first in 1967 by Éditions Romanes, 'restored and adapted to the French language from a Cabalistic manuscript', and its working part has been reprinted in the modern French edition of *Asia Mysteriosa*, published by Janvier in 1995 and Pardes in 1997. It is, I believe, of very uncertain provenance and should not be used as the foundation for fanciful theories, although the Oracle itself is interesting.

scribed Father Julian as being one of three 'Little Lights of the
Orient', but who were the other two? Although a hierarchy of
Wise Ones is described, the regular communicators are shown
to be Julian himself (the primary voice), and a Master with the
Tibetan name, 'Tek the Wise'. The third member of the Little
Lights is not named. The Oracle uses a luminous phrase to describe the three of them: 'The Three Wise Ones are the Little
Lights who live far from all and near to all'. At pains always
to show the universality of the Oracle's teaching, Bhotiva then
gives many other examples of threefold spiritual beings. The
philosophy of *Asia Mysteriosa* might be described as syncretic
(it would say 'synthetic') meaning simply that it brings traditions
into synthesis, rather than separates them out. There is also a
mysterious being who seems to be beyond and outside the three,
who is simply referred to as 'He who Waits'. There has been
much speculation about this being, whom I shall discuss later.

We know from the Polaire *Bulletins* that the Oracle gave its
inner group a Star symbol, an open star with six points. This
symbol was to hold a central place on every cover of the *Bulletin*, even every time the cover design changed (which was annu-
ally) and when it became bimonthly in 1934, changing its name
to *Les Cahiers de la Fraternité Polaire*. I have not actually
seen an issue after the first issue of 1934, but I have seen reference to issues as late as 1937. We must see the 1920s as a time
when the small group was forming under this symbol. Their concentration was upon the essence of the messages from the Wise
Ones, and the bringing to humanity of the true meaning of the
Star.* We do not know much about those who formed the core
save that they called themselves 'La Racine' (the Root or Stem)*

*The best evidence of this is the extraordinary tokens of recognition
exchanged between Bhotiva and my grandparents when they met for the
first time in January 1931, described in ARTHUR CONAN DOYLE'S BOOK OF THE
BEYOND, pp. 23–5 and 85–6. White Eagle had been teaching about the Star
all through the 1920s, just as had the Oracle, and the White Eagle Lodge
continues the work of focus upon the light of the Star to this day.

but also enjoyed thinking of themselves as the five petals of the rose, at the other end of the stem. The five-petalled rose symbol is significant in any ideas we might have about the composition and number of this group. From among it, only the names of Fille and Bhotiva are certain; there are others we might guess.

The *Petites Lumières*, the Little Lights, seem to have taken on the mantle of the Rosicrucian 'Wise Knights initiated into the Great Wheel' (p. 145). Guénon's withdrawn Preface was much taken up with a discussion of how supposedly Himalayan Masters might use a Western, perhaps Rosicrucian, vocabulary and mindset. He satisfied himself within the context of his Preface, and yet his falling out with his Polaire friends lay with his attempt to check whether the Little Lights read Sanskrit.†

But at this mention of the Rosicrucians, let *Asia Mysteriosa* take up the story. 'In June or July 1929 we received, thanks always to the Oracle of Astral Force, a certain number of communications referring to the formation, or rather the re-formation, of a Group called the "Polaires".' This was a 'reconstruction', *Asia Mysteriosa* affirms, inasmuch as it links straight back to the '"Wise Knights" who, around the end of the seventeenth century, withdrew, "taken over by the Little Lights of the East", to the snowy and invulnerable peaks of the Himalaya'. Taking the term to apply to a single individual, Ivan Cooke, in THY KINGDOM COME, is certain that the true Wise Knight or Chevalier Sage is one and the same with the Theosophical Master 'R', the Comte de St-Germain.# There is a little confusion between *Asia Mysteriosa* and the **Bulletin** here, since the latter refers to the Polaires' predecessors being scattered at the end of the *fifteenth* century, 'by the base speculation of men and by fear of the true light'.§ The later date would see the Rosicrucians

*For La Racine, see below, pp. 29–31, and **Bulletin**. †See below, pp. 8, 16 and 26. #Or see ARTHUR CONAN DOYLE'S BOOK OF THE BEYOND, pp. 88–9. §*Asia Mysteriosa*, 1929, has the phrase 'La peur de la Lumière' but the promotional Bulletin (i.e., the reprint of the May 1930 one, has this full phrase, 'la peur de la véritable Lumière'. See also pp. 34–5, below.

through to the formation of the Royal Society in England but not much after; the earlier date would fit with the generally supposed time of Christian Rosenkreutz himself.

Asia Mysteriosa continues:

'This is the first communication, completely unexpected in fact, in which we found information concerning the "Polaires":

'Form the Group of "Polaires" and spread it throughout the World – following the indications that will be given to you – on the following theme: Light on Spiritualism.'

Another great surprise for the small group of friends who had worked together through the 1920s! The Oracle was no longer giving them wise advice, it was prompting them to action. After this message, 'for one and a half months the operator – as if animated by a new fervour – worked to obtain replies concerning the Group of "Polaires". Some of them were very long (we received one containing 280 words) and this vast work is not yet finished'.

Our story is getting curiouser and curiouser, as Alice would say. A spiritual group led by an Oracle; reference back to an occult initiative years before. Yet we have already heard how Father Julian 'undoubtedly had the sign of the Rose Cross under his cloak', so the Rosicrucian link should not surprise us. As to the relevance of Spiritualism, we need both to broaden our reference and to refresh our understanding of the 1930s.

*

In fact, our look at the 'Thirties', as we will loosely call the ten years between *Asia Mysteriosa*'s publication and the outbreak of World War II, is long overdue. First, if we are going to understand the Polaires and their ideals, we somehow need to see the Thirties in their own right, not through the screen of World War II, and certainly not through the Holocaust. With hindsight, we can see the warning signs; we cannot however expect those who lived in the Thirties to have had that perspective. By contrast, World War I was a recent memory for all but the youngest generation and for many in France, at least, the heart of the conflict in Europe was seen as France's ancient rivalry with Germany – something which had led in 1870 and again in 1914 to a war fought on French soil. What today we would call 'hawks' in France saw the need to punish Germany with huge reparations, something France's allies in part resisted. Here is not the place to discuss the effect the Versailles Treaty and its aftermath had on German politics, but they have been endlessly discussed by historians of the rise of Hitler. To place *Asia Mysteriosa* in time it is certainly as well to remember that in 1929 we are exactly midway between the publication of MEIN KAMPF and Hitler's coming to power in 1933. This date is of course crucial; from that moment, the atmosphere darkened in Europe; what was intellectually safe in 1929 was considerably less safe after 1933. Otto Rahn, author of CRUSADE AGAINST THE GRAIL (in German, 1933; in French, 1934) was a friend of some of the Polaires and possibly a Polaire himself; back in Germany, he was snapped up by Himmler as a probing archaeologist who might further the Nazi search for historical identity. The Polaires were surely watched.

Both France and Germany nonetheless owed their general sense of identity to a time when they formed part of the same empire under Charlemagne, eleven hundred years earlier. A 'dovish' position, we might almost say an altruistic one, might therefore have lain in bringing the countries together in unity or even union. It is precisely this sort of aspect of history that is so easily lost when we take a look back through what happened after, just as it is tempting a few years later to launder out of history the numbers in Britain who pursued an appeasement policy, yet this search for an unlikely union at the heart of Europe lies at the root of the European Union today.

I have used the term 'altruistic'; it may too general a term, but in the 1929 context it is also important to remember that the whole of Europe, exhausted by conflict, sought solutions to the problems of national rivalry and human enmity. This is no less true in the esoteric or occult world than in politics (wherein the

League of Nations is the most obvious example). It is therefore
also possible to see the Thirties as a time of enormous idealism set against a ferment of ideas. Poets of the Thirties bring us
radical Socialist utopias, after years when otherwise respectable
English intellectuals are tainted by theories of eugenics. Psy-
chologists search concepts such as the herd instinct for the causes of human division, or find interim answers in opposing character types. Experimental communities of all types are established.
Idealism of an only slightly different sort will drive men in the
direction of secret societies. Other human beings will be driven
to new religions. Swami Vivekananda's appearance at the World
Parliament of Religions in Chicago in 1893 had brought a new
respect for Hinduism, particularly Vedanta, that continued for
decades. Krishnamurti was promoted as a new World Teacher by
the Theosophists in the 1920s; in the same year as *Asia Mysteriosa* appeared, he refused that role and dissolved the Order
of the Star. Among the new teachers from India, via America,
Paramahansa Yogananda was a visitor to many countries in Europe in 1935 and to England again in 1936. Maurice Magre (as
himself, certainly not as René Thimmy!), had written POURQUOI JE
SUIS BOUDDHISTE ('Why I am a Buddhist') in 1928.

   In fact, Madame Blavatsky's Theosophy, which goes back well
into the previous century, is crucial to the understanding of much
of the esoteric movement, the Polaires and Guénon included.
Her finest disciple, Annie Besant, died in 1930. Theosophy had
resurrected a myth – the Hyperborean or Aryan myth – that was
to inspire groups and individuals whom today we would quickly
divide into 'bad' (the search for racial purity, fed by the Nazi psychology) or relatively 'good' (idealisms seeking to bring human
beings together in brotherhood under a strong sense of values).

   Somewhere in this myth, too, lies a special icon, the place
known as Agartha. There is major confusion between this place
and Shambhala, another legendary city, which features particularly strongly in Vajrayana and Tibetan Buddhism and also in

Theosophy. Traditionally, Shambala is a place of beauty while Agartha is a subterranean land populated by demons, but writers just before *Asia Mysteriosa* had managed to transpose the two, so that Agartha is the abode of the Masters. A key source for *Asia Mysteriosa* is the work of the occultist Alexandre Saint-Yves d'Alveydre (1842–1909). Saint-Yves claimed a personal revelation for his elaborate account of the fabled Agartha, here a location for wisdom and spiritual direction. The idea was developed by Réné Guénon in LE ROI DU MONDE ('The King of the World', 1927).* *Asia Mysteriosa*'s Little Lights communicate from Himalayan retreats, not necessarily underground, but mysterious and remote from the eyes of men.

Saint-Yves also conjured a term, 'synarchy', as the opposite to anarchy. Where anarchy posits no rule among men, synarchy is 'the association of everyone with everyone else' and a bringing together, in the process, of culture, religion and politics. Attractive though the idea might seem in theory, in practice it is perilously poised between impossible idealism on the one side and the alarming concept of unelected world government on the other. There is no mention at all of synarchy in *Asia Mysteriosa*, but the idea was to affect the later Polaires and may therefore wrongly colour our ideas about the original small group who were behind *Asia Mysteriosa*. Even synarchy needs to be seen in the context of the desire to bring Europe together peacefully (above, p. 21). The notes to *Asia Mysteriosa* however present us with a lively list of figures, some of whom, though they were maybe less controversial in 1929, have acquired a certain notoriety through subsequent history: men such as Julius Evola and even Jean

---

*Other key figures to write about Agartha include Ferdynand Ossendowski mentioned several times in *Asia Mysteriosa*, and Louis Jacolliot. For analysis of the huge literature around similar ideas, see Joscelyn Godwin, ARKTOS (Kempton, IL: Adventures Unlimited, 1996). Guénon's LE ROI DU MONDE will have been seminal, particularly since it was so contemporary, but for some doubts about Guénon's disinterestedness, see Marco Baistrocchi, 'Agarttha: a Guénonian Manipulation', in *Theosophical History*, Occasional Papers XII, December 2009.

Marquès-Rivière, one of those who wrote a preface to the work here, both of them very tied to a right wing agenda. The Polaire who believed in the group's articles of faith truly had no politics.* The Thirties positively teem with esoteric groups. LA MAGIE À PARIS and LES SOCIÉTÉS SECRÈTES À PARIS, already mentioned, give a maybe over-colourful account of Parisian ones and include the Polaires. However in England, in the years following World War I, it is Spiritualism that most strikingly features in the world of non-traditional religious thought and philosophy. Two features undoubtedly drive this. First, there is the tremendous loss – almost the loss of a generation – in the double tragedy of the war and the influenza epidemic that followed it. Second, there is the hopelessness of the Depression and the opportunity that a higher spiritual world offered as an escape. Neither of these influences belittle Spiritualism, out of which my own spiritual tradition, the White Eagle Lodge, largely came in 1936– but they do in part explain the huge numbers Spiritualism could draw to its cause.

Spiritualism has generally sat more easily with the British mind than the French. Even the word used is not quite the same, the French preferring 'Spiritisme', which was the word coined by its early French codifier and systematizer, Allan Kardec (1804–69). He created something unique: a follower, Camille Flammarion, was able to write: 'Spiritism is not a religion but a science'. When the founding instructions to the Polaires included an investigation of 'Spiritualism', it is likely that a much broader philosophical topic, the study of things of the spirit, their primacy, and their interaction with matter, is meant. Although English Spiritualism attracted several first-class scientific minds such as Sir Oliver Lodge and Sir William Crookes, and good literary minds like Sir Arthur Conan Doyle's, relative to the rational French approach its appeal was

*The Polaires were clear, however, that a second World War was approaching. See *Asia Mysteriosa*, below, p. 132, and ARTHUR CONAN DOYLE'S BOOK OF THE BEYOND, pp. 35–6. Correspondence between Grace Cooke and Jean Conan Doyle in 1930 also covered this topic (papers in the Harry Ransom Center, Univ. Texas).

sentimental. And there was therefore in England a great search for proof, which endless writers and experimenters claimed to have found, none of them to be universally believed. It was Sir Arthur Conan Doyle's Spiritualism that brought together my grandmother and the Polaires, shortly after his death in 1930; no one more than he longed for this proof 'to crash all critics'.*

Just what lies behind the theme given the Polaires for their work, described as 'Light on Spiritualism', we shall probably never fully know, though *Asia Mysteriosa* has plenty of hints when the word is taken with its wider meaning, as opposed to the context of English Spiritualism. The links the Polaires made with my grandmother after Sir Arthur's death, even though the instruction to make the link came via the Oracle, led to enormous antagonisms within Polaire ranks, so great was French suspicion of the subject: a regular insistence in the *Bulletin* is that 'Les Polaires ne sont pas des Spirites': 'the Polaires are not Spiritualists'.†

If there was antagonism to Spiritualism in the narrow sense, we need to remember that they still saw death as one of the things most affecting 'sorrowing humanity'. The other great Polaire charge, given in the Appendix to *Asia Mysteriosa*, was that of helping humanity overcome 'the mad fear of death'. I have written about this elsewhere.#

*

After they received the instruction from the Oracle to 'Form the Group of "Polaires"', the Racine group did just as they were told. Fernand Divoire, editor of a leading evening newspaper and already mentioned as the author of a preface, was known or introduced to the group at this time and to explore the Oracle he set up a trial of the method in the presence of journalists and men of letters (Geyraud, SOCIÉTÉS SECRÈTES, p. 60). From this

*The phrase is actually Bhotiva's, though it appealed greatly to Ivan Cooke: see ARTHUR CONAN DOYLE'S BOOK OF THE BEYOND, p. 117.

†E.g. in the *Bulletin* of October 1931, p. 3.

#See 'Cathar Joy' in THE CATHAR VIEW (London: Polair, 2012), pp. 11–23. For 'the mad fear', see below, p. 158, and the Polaire *Bulletin* of 9 May 1930.

and a number of other sources we might start to build up a list
of persons interested in the Polaire work. Divoire provided the
group's first home, in his offices, and undoubtedly gave the en-
deavour a huge boost by the support his printing house offered.

Soon, though, the Polaires had a problem. Enquiries were coming in, apparently in their thousands. The *Bulletins* of August
and September 1930 talk of the countries in the world to which
the work has spread, and how from early 1931 there will be editions of the *Bulletin* in English, Spanish and Portuguese.The first
issue of the *Bulletin* was reprinted again and again as a promo-
tion, and in October 1930 a special card with a silver six-pointed
star was sent out. By February 1931 100,000 pieces of publicity
had been sent out. In August 1930 the group announced its new
home, 36 Avenue Junot, in the 18th *arrondisement*. Yet there is
strife noted, too. The November 1930 *Bulletin* answers an at-
tack in the October *Revue Internationale des Sociétés Secrètes*, and
the spat with René Guénon continued when he attacked them in
February 1931 in *La Voile d'Isis*. It was lamented that Guénon's
article affected Lady Conan Doyle's collaboration in the work just
mentioned, and the March 1931 *Bulletin* published the preface
to *Asia* Guénon had written and then withdrawn. By then its author was in Cairo, never to return. Yet there was ever a weakness for the Polaires. Whatever the success of *Asia* as a piece of
writing (and Thimmy says it only sold to 'the curious'), the whole
justification for the Polaire work and the direction it took lay with
the Oracle. So each one in the long list of subscribers, as well as
uncommitted outsiders yet to choose their path, quite reasonably
must have wanted to know the nature of the Oracle and how it
worked. If *Asia Mysteriosa* satisfied, well and good. If it did not,
there was little other authority to which to appeal.

Since the instruction to Mario, by the hermit, was that he
should reveal the secret of the operation to no one, then whatever *Asia Mysteriosa* tells us, it must convince us but not give
away the secret. It must be a fountain of both information and

disinformation. All *Asia Mysteriosa* could do was demonstrate the method and the intellectual context in which the Oracle existed, the wisdom and accuracy of its answers, the level of research which backed up its use, and the number of intellectual authorities who had accredited it through actual trial.

If it has been treated dismissively in more recent times, we must therefore in part blame the impossibility of the writers' task. We may also need partly to blame ourselves and our desire for quick answers. The Oracle is intended to give answers, but it is not intended to be a gimmick. When it was offered a flippant question, it refused to deal with it. The phrasing of the question was a careful art. And then you left it, till the answer came back. *Asia Mysteriosa* deserves the same respect – not because it is right or wrong, but because if we approach it wrongly, we shall misundertand it. Nowhere is this more apparent than in the answer it gave to René Guénon which so offended him. Here it is, as recorded by René Thimmy (p. 166).

'He wanted to put the oracle to the test: to set, by the way of questions he asked of it, a kind of examination for the three sages in their faraway home.

'Can we set an exam for the wise holders of the truth, for the masters who inhabit the solitudes of Tibet? This is a delicate problem.

'The answers to the first two issues were, I believe, deemed satisfactory by René Guénon. The three sages were well taught by wise men, by real wise men. But he set a trap for them. He wanted to be sure of their knowledge of Sanskrit.

'What is Hamsa?' he asked them, finally.

'Hamsa means the symbolic swan and also the liberation of the spirit. But did the wise men know this?

'The answer was enigmatic and could not, in any aspect that we should consider, be seen as contemptful of the questioner. It was roughly as follows:

'Smoke hemp root from a water pipe and you'll know what Hamsa is.'

Poor René Guénon: made fun of by a mathematical method. But the more one considers this answer, the deeper it is. First of all, it is reasonable to say that to understand *hamsa* you have to experience it, not just be told about it. Taking drugs may be a cheap short cut, but it probably gets the subject closer to understanding than the mind ever will. So secondly, I believe the Oracle is saying to Guénon, 'Get out of the mind that traps you: life will teach you liberation, not books'.

Most readers will see **Asia Mysteriosa** materialistically, purely as a way of getting an answer to a question. This is precisely the practice around which the Oracle offers the most cautions, however. Its instructions insist that the questioning must arise out of what Geyraud (p. 57) calls 'grave doubt' but might be better thought of as deep contemplation, in other words that an enormous amount of attention must go into how the question is put (p. 142, the answer from 'Anselm' which leads to the apology, 'the interested party … admitted having asked this question without concentrating and very rapidly, and he insisted writing it in this way as an experiment'), and so on. The materialistic view also misses the depth of reference that *Asia Mysteriosa* has in Buddhist and other thought. To witness this, see the discussion of the concept of **moksha** (albeit contributed by Jean Marquès-Rivière) on pp. 137–8, or the rather beautiful writing about Anand, or *ananda*, on pp. 139–40, including a comparison of Ananda with St John, the Beloved of Jesus, as specially regarded pupils of their teacher. *Asia Mysteriosa* is about a path to God, or what some might call spiritual freedom, not about getting one's career in shape, although there are some interesting answers given to 'career' questions. Or take the following footnotes which together make a point-by-point commentary on the 'preface' dictated by the sage, Tek the Wise:

(1) Evolution through pain. It is in the trial of pain that men transform themselves and evolve towards a superior spirituality.

(2) It is as if these sparks were insufficiently retained in their physical receptacle, the human body.

(3) The return to God. This is the Paradise of various religions, while Purgatory would correspond to survival in other worlds.

(4) This sentence, well worthy of the philosophy of those who have no material connections, indicates that our struggles for life here below are useless and it would be preferable to orientate all our efforts towards spiritual refinement; whereas the return to God is by our "always greater" dreams and ambitions and the struggles they inevitably create, we prepare for ourselves a long series of existences before attaining the indefinable level.

René Guénon was one of the founders of the school of Traditionalism in esotericism, philosophy and anthropology. He argued that it was impossible to understand the subtle thought behind any kind of belief without actually being part of the tradition in which the belief was cradled. Despite Guénon's break with the Polaires, it is precisely to Guénon that I would turn to insist that understanding of *Asia Mysteriosa* will only come when there is true sympathy with it. *Asia Mysteriosa* is a generous document that repays not only intellectual attention, but the suspension of the intellect when required. And as a meditation teacher I am aware of how many tricks we need to have at our disposal to get the mind out of the way, if we are indeed to perceive intuitive truth – something the rational mind can never quite do.

Once we respect the spirituality of *Asia Mysteriosa*, it comes to life. We find that the phrase already quoted from the late *Bulletins*, 'The replies burst forth, surprisingly accurate and illuminated by the most ineffable goodness and the most noble spirituality', rings true. We also do best to remember the original Racine or 'root' group, who did not 'go public' with the Oracle until they had instruction to do so, and had been working with it for most of the 1920s, and isolate them in our minds from the large outer, and often later, group whose own mental vibrations changed the Polaires, narrowed the ideals (the powerful focus of which is evident in (3) and (4) in the notes just quoted), and led it in various different directions, none of them holding to the centre. In THY KINGDOM COME Ivan Cooke always speaks respectfully of the early Polaires whom he knew, and even in 1938, after a full break had occurred between the Cookes and the Polaires, in a manuscript history of the English White Eagle Brotherhood which is almost certainly by him, he is still reverential of their integrity in two eloquent phrases:

'The Polaire Brotherhood at its prime formed a body of men and women strongly linked to a great Source of spiritual power, and with each Brother attuned or linked to the other, by a method unpractised since early Egypt.'

'There can be no question of the purity of motive, service and sacrifice given in those early days.'*

As late as 1971, he wrote of the Oracle:

'Lengthy experience has since convinced us both of its truth and accuracy, and given us considerable respect for any messages coming from the Sages.... Its messages to our knowledge were always true, to the point, terse and vivid.'†

Lastly, here is Grace Cooke, writing in 1946 of her first exposure to the Polaire 'magic' at the Stead Library. 'Z' is M. Bhotiva:

'The power which manifested during that evening in Mr. Stead's study when I first met 'Z' can only be described as a supreme spiritual experience. It was my first contact with the power of the Sages and their representative. My mind was raised far beyond my normal consciousness to a condition of limitless time and space, in which I contacted some eternal life-stream. I no longer felt imprisoned in the little personality of my present life, but was travelling in a timeless sea wherein my past, present and future merged into one stream.#

*The manuscript history is in the White Eagle Lodge archives.
†ARTHUR CONAN DOYLE'S BOOK OF THE BEYOND, p. 56.
#THE SHINING PRESENCE, p. 26. London: White Eagle Lodge, 1936.

One thing we learn from this is about the power of the Polaires as meditators, which may be a clue to understanding our present text. Reading of their ability to attune themselves to each other in the way Ivan Cooke describes, and hearing of their integrity, we may find it easier imaginatively to comprehend the intimacy that the Racine group had with the Oracle and the teachers behind it. It is not clear to whom the reply which begins 'Imperfect but beloved son' (p. 136) is addressed; perhaps to Mario Fille himself. Mario seems at one point to have asked,

QUESTION: May I have direct communication with you?
REPLY: By refining the spirit, by abandoning all material things. Then ask and you will have the reply through inspiration.

The response is that of the real spiritual teacher, and the group, in these moments, are true pupils. Maybe this is the strongest clue we are given as to how to understand *Asia Mysteriosa*. For as we get to know them, real characters emerge from these pages. Mario must have been maddening to work with, as is evidenced by the story (pp. 63–4) about his friends asking endless questions about the Oracle at the beginning, and him responding with nothing but 'yes' or 'no' answers. Then they found a way round him, and went straight to the Oracle. It's a nice little insight, and it offers no excuse for commentators to belittle the group, as they have loved to do.

That Fille and Bhotiva were members of the original group is reasonable assumption, but we do not specifically know who else the Racine comprised; true Polaires were secret about their initiation. But we know some of those who were close. Maurice Magre wrote frequently for the *Bulletin*, and despite the popularising irreverence of his remarks in LA MAGIE À PARIS, was famous for his colourful sexual adventures and his experiments with opium. That doesn't make him the perfect candidate to leave the incarnational cycle, but it does humanise him, and the group generally. Otto Rahn, at the opposite extreme, whom

I believe to have been a Polaire, was intense and deeply idealistic, homosexual in an age of persecution, half-Jewish in a nation that had turned against its Jewry. If he allowed himself to get caught up in Nazism – and he may very possibly have been forced in – one thing we can say is that it was a total perversion of the group's ideals, and he seems to have regretted it horribly.

For a perception of Bhotiva, we might turn to Ivan Cooke and THY KINGDOM COME again, but the most evocative account is in Grace Cooke's own memoir, THE SHINING PRESENCE (p. 29). 'How can I describe him,' she asks, 'One of the two most remarkable men I have ever met?'

'He was of the Latin type, medium in height, broad-shouldered, lithe, active and forceful. His hair and eyes were dark, almost black I think; his features regular, with something of that command one sees occasionally in the portraits of an emperor of long ago – indeed he was an Italian by birth I understood. These words give but a poor indication of the quality of the man. Someone who once saw him at a London terminus said that, although he was unobtrusively dressed and bore himself modestly, he stood out from the throng like a king. As I came to know him better I found he had an understanding far in advance of most other mortals; he could be gentle as a child, sympathetic and kindly, and yet, on occasion, displayed an energy and resolution almost terrifying. I recognised a spiritual insight, an intuition that made each word he spoke worthy of remembrance and careful weighing. We worked together for some years. Throughout this time he never wavered in the respect he showed to White Eagle, to whom, from the first, he accorded something akin to reverence.'

Such is an indication of the broad spread of personalities of the group, and of Fille we know perhaps the least. They were idealistic human beings, of good intellect but initially little 'savvy' in the ways of the world, and soon their group which had grown so fast was becoming too much to hold, a sort of Pygmalion. Yet once the perception is distorted, all sorts of assertions creep in. For some writers since those times, 'He who Waits' must surely be Hitler – for little better reason than that the date 1933 seems somehow linked with the manifestation of the mysterious avatar. It makes no sense; how does such a reader explain the association of 'He who Waits' with Ananda, the disciple of Buddha, on pp. 139–40, and by total contrast who does the same reader think is identified in the discussion of the fearful *kala-nag* (pp. 132–3), if indeed anyone is?

To be fair, *Asia Mysteriosa* does contradict itself by allowing some discussion of personalities against that strange 'He who Waits' sobriquet. Presumably, Krishnamurti was introduced by a questioner in the belief he might be just that teacher – the Oracle's negative response causes the modern reader to blush, and I cannot quite explain the strength of feeling (p. 131). Followers of Omraam Mikhaël Aïvanhov have tried to indicate their guru as 'He who Waits', reissuing *Asia Mysteriosa* as LUMIÈRE DE SHAMBHALA in 1995 (Editions Télésma). But a much more satisfying clue to 'He who Waits' is provided by the instruction on p. 117, '*Work with determination and tenacity until you are acquainted with He Who Waits...*' and phrases, albeit from as early as 1925, to the effect '*Many, many moons will pass before you meet He Who Waits...*'. Alongside a discussion of He who Waits as possibly 'the manifestation of the Word at the end of the present Cycle or Manvantara', we are on much securer ground if we see this being as one to be realised, first, through our inner aspiration, maybe in meditation, whether or not he/she is destined to manifest on earth.

In this connection we might note again the quiet comparison made soon after the mention of Ananda, with the 'beloved disciple' of Jesus, who is St John. Magre and Rahn were both passionately interested in the Cathars of the Languedoc, for whom St John's Gospel was absolutely paramount. When my grandmother travelled to the area with the Polaires in 1931, she had an experience of profound connection with St John there,

and White Eagle, her guide, constantly identifies St John with
the Master of the New Age. *Asia Mysteriosa* carries frequent
reference to the Sun God, Apollo, and beneath an excursus on
this, a footnote on p. 82 mentions 'the solar role attributed by
the Cathars to arithmetic (illuminated Reason), as a comment
to the phrase 'the symbolic leitmotif of communications (from
the Oracle of Astral Force) is based on Light and on Sun.' In
1929 Bhotiva and other Polaires had yet to travel to Cathar
country, but already sensed, maybe with the help of Maurice
Magre, the special importance the Cathar heretics had for their
own unorthodox beliefs, and in the reference quoted show obvious special reverence for St John too.

*

One last point needs to be made. It is about a phrase used both
in *Asia Mysteriosa* and in the *Bulletin* about the reason for the
dispersal of the Rosicrucians. It is 'the fear of the true light', *la
véritable Lumière* (see p. 20). I don't claim fully to be able to explain this phrase, but it recurs in Bhotiva's correspondence with
my grandmother, some of which I have quoted in ARTHUR CONAN
DOYLE'S BOOK OF THE BEYOND. One way in which I possibly understand it *viz -à-viz* my grandmother's lack of fear is the sense I
always had around her, that if spirit gave her a clear direction to
do something, she did it without question and however bizarre
it seemed. Thus in 1945, almost without any funds of her own

---

*The vision she had is described in THE LIVING WORD (London: White Eagle
Publications, first edition 1949) and there is further information about St John in
another White Eagle book, THE LIGHT BRINGER (Liss, Hants.: White Eagle Publishing Trust, 2000). There is a certain amount of disinformation about this trip in
print. It undoubtedly took place in July 1931, with both Grace and Ivan Cooke
present, and there was no follow-up to it, despite a story that begins in Walter
Birks' biographical writing that Ivan Cooke went back in 1932 (Birks, Walter,
and Gilbert, R. A., THE TREASURE OF MONTSÉGUR, London, 1987). Nor do I think it
is true to say that those who went came back empty-handed – and certainly not
without knowing for certain what they hoped to find. I have set out a fuller argument in 'A Trip to Ariège in 1931' in THE CATHAR VIEW, pp. 173–86; my grandmother's vision is reprinted in the same book (pp.143–7).

and incurring huge debts to friends, she purchased both a country centre for the White Eagle Lodge and took out a mortgage to acquire its London premises, simply because such was the instruction given her. Fear of the true light is exactly what she encountered from 'sensible' people all around: but her direction was spirit's, not theirs. The true light, I would suggest, is what spirit actually states, not what we would like to believe it said.

We may recognise the same unquestioning observance lurking in Bhotiva too, to judge from the account of him we have just had from my grandmother. Similarly, although I rely on anecdotal evidence I can even less substantiate here, the character of Mario Fille was such that he would obey the Oracle absolutely without question, if its response was clear enough. As I understand it, it was the tendency of others to put their own judgment before the advice of their Eastern teachers that caused the initial members of the Polaire group progressively to withdraw and quietly let their enthusiastic colleagues do what they wanted while continuing what we might call the 'inner' work on their own.

'Fear of the true light' was clearly an iconic phrase, one maybe originating from the Oracle itself, and it is one hint we have that whatever we pick up from *Asia Mysteriosa* that there is something more we may need to understand, about both the Rosicrucians and the Polaires, something we are not fully being told. *Asia Mysteriosa* seems to take us just so far, but only hint at what is yet to come.* It is one reason why I have recommended close but meditative absorption of the text. 'Never trust the teller, trust the tale', to quote D. H. Lawrence.

*

So how are we, finally, to understand *Asia Mysteriosa*? First, I think we have to remember it as exactly what it was, not so much an explanation, but the opening of a quest. It is almost as though understanding the Oracle is a challenge we are being

*The second book, promised in *Asia Mysteriosa* on p. 154, never appeared.

set – with a goal of spiritual wisdom at the end of it. Secondly, I believe, we will always be closer to *Asia Mysteriosa* when we are asking questions (and hearing the responses inwardly as well as outwardly) than when we think we have answers. Answers crystallise and restrict, whereas questions, in this sort of instance, keep the mind open. Thus we might ask, alongside the question just posed about 'the true light':

¶ What is the real truth behind the somewhat unlikely story of the chance meeting between the hermit and the boy in 1908?

¶ What was the point of doing these incredibly complicated arithmetical calculations, and how was it the answers touched their listeners so deeply when they came by such a method?

¶ What do Bhotiva's Hinduism and Magre's Buddhism, and their apparent ability in meditation, tell us, at a period in history when both systems of thought were the preserve of so few?

¶ How do we best understand *Asia Mysteriosa* in the context of the long list of ideals of the Polaires, dominated by combatting 'egotism' and 'the mad fear of death', set out in the first *Bulletin* and in almost identical form at the end of *Asia Mysteriosa* (pp. 157–8, below)?

¶ Why were so many people of intellectual stature so impressed by the Oracle, and how do we understand the very sensitive appreciation they voiced?

¶ What was it that the Polaires saw and understood in the Cathars or Albigenses, and does it link to Rosicrucianism or not?

¶ Why was understanding 'Spiritualism', albeit with the meaning defined above, such an important mission for them?

¶ What would be the outcome of meditating on the following statement by the Oracle (*Asia Mysteriosa*, p. 141)?

In the true Life of Light there must be no duality. There is only infinite love in all and for all. The most perfect, by Divine Will, can have missions.

Colum Hayward, London, September 2012

Asia Mysteriosa

(ASIA THE MYSTERIOUS)

The Oracle of Astral Force
as a means of communication with
'The Little Lights of the East'

PRECEDED BY A PREFACE BY
FERNAND DIVOIRE
AND ESSAYS BY MAURICE MAGRE
AND JEAN MARQUES-RIVIERE

PREFACE

It was perhaps by chance that, one day, I came to meet the promoter of this Method. We talked, bound by a common curiosity and by common concerns. It had not occurred to me to disbelieve the story of Father Julian any more than I disbelieve fairy tales. All that is necessary is to understand.

Then, with this promoter, I met the one who holds the precious manuscript and asked questions. I kept up these questions, and the answers were at once coherent, revelatory and obscure. Clearly obscure, so to speak. After various experiments, some of which were conducted in private, I came to certain preliminary conclusions, as follows:

1)   The Method exists.

2)   The Method was not invented by its current keeper.

3)   The keeper is honest and impartial.

4)   The keeper is a man without any spiritual prejudice and who, consequently, has no philosophical interest in falsifying or 'imposing' a reply.

5)   The answers obtained by the Method are in no way clairvoyant prophecies but, on the contrary, general views, intelligent words and wise, affectionate advice.

6)   The Method seems rigorously mathematical and the keeper seems to content himself with applying mathematic rules exactly as a calculating machine would.

I can go no further than the word 'seem', for the extraordinary dovetailing of certain answers to certain questions remains, for me, mysterious.

The calculator consciously contents himself with counting, without intervening in any way in his operations or in their results; what I do not know is if *unconsciously* he does not receive a sort of strange dictation, if some intelligence outside himself does not intervene in his calculations.

I do not affirm, I do not know, and I see full well that the Method is purely arithmetical, but I still come away from it with a sense of mystery.

FERNAND DIVOIRE

A MEANS OF COMMUNICATION
WITH THE MASTERS

AN ESSAY BY MAURICE MAGRE

I believe that all dreams, after they have started out as dreams, end up by becoming realities. In the mould of creative thought, facts come together quite obediently, plausibly and harmoniously—so strange is the shifting world we have invented. One must dream beautiful stories if life is to become beautiful.

In addition, the usual manner of thinking in men of my time seems to me absurd, erroneous and unwise. We begin by not believing, by demanding proof, and by scoffing at that which is new.

Travellers who have discovered the world have ended their lives in bitterness for this reason. Accounts of their adventurous travels have met with only scepticism among the sedentary people to whom they have returned. Marco Polo convinced the Venetians that he had stayed in Asia only by showing them precious stones he had brought back. Bruce was the legend of London because of his so-called lies about Ethiopia. A few days ago I met a born non-believer who questioned Madame David-Neel's extraordinary journey on foot in Tibet.

I think one must be anti-scientific and clearly adopt the way of gullibility. Through faith we give complete value to an invention or to an account of things and we benefit from its value as novelty. We receive richness from it. There is

plenty of time afterwards to use the touchstone of reasonable reflection, and to consider whether or not its elements
are false, and we run the risk, at times, of transforming
fiction into fact by the strength of our faith.

A little of this spontaneous faith is needed to read this
book and study the absolutely marvellous divination
method it sets out. Can something that is really marvellous possibly be worthless? What our fathers attributed
to divine or demonic influences now appears to us as the
play of natural forces. Every day these forces receive an
astounding application. Yet men, stubbornly confined in
their desire to doubt, set the most obstinate negation upon
all that has not received an official stamp or not been ap-
proved by some Academy or launched at Ministerial level.

To me it seems in no way extraordinary to be able to
communicate with individuals living in the Himalaya by a
method based on numbers and to receive from these very
wise beings guidance on life, philosophical glimpses of the
world and partial prediction of the future. Armed with the
undoubted good faith of those who bring me this method,
I am delighted to have been led to their path. There I find
confirmation of my personal ideas concerning a community of men who are more enlightened than we are, who have
reached one degree higher up the evolutionary scale and
who live in the solitude of Tibet, working for the general
good, within the limits of their power—which is greater
than ours but still limited. In any case I can see no reason
for me to disbelieve an affirmation presented completely
unselfishly and which teaches the highest moral doctrine.

The existence of this Brotherhood, called alternately
'Agartha' and 'the Great White Lodge', has been known

for a very long time, yet without having been proven by the 'material evidence' for which the Western mind hungers. It was to reach this Brotherhood that Apollonius of Tyana went to India, to the mountains 'where the trees have blue apples, like the calyx of the hyacinth'. It was they who gave him the mission for which he travelled the shores of the Mediterranean, and the Brotherhood which led him to say: 'I always remember my Masters and I travel the world teaching what I have learnt from them'.

We know almost nothing about Christian Rosenkreutz beyond that he went to the East in search of the message of truth; he seems to have set out from his Monastery in Germany solely to communicate with the Masters whose existence he knew of from an ancient tradition and whose messengers he was to meet in Damascus.

In the seventeenth century the traveller Paul Lucas, in charge of archaeological research in Syria and Palestine for Louis XIV, reported, with reference to Nicolas Flamel, a conversation he supposedly had in Broussa* with scholars and Eastern philosophers. They are reported to have confirmed to him that there was, somewhere, to the north of India, a Centre from which initiates set out and returned once their task was completed.

Many other words have been reported and many other traditions have affirmed the existence of the Himalayan Spiritual Centre, but what makes this existence absolutely certain in my mind is the founding in 1875 by Madame Blavatsky of the Theosophical movement. Two Hindus, Koot Hoomi and Moriah, living in seclusion in a Tibetan lamasery, taught her and gave her the mission of spread-

*In Turkey.

ing the essential ideas of their philosophy in the West.
From the information they gave her, she wrote 'The Secret
Doctrine', in which can be found—on the origin of the
world, planetary and human evolution, life after death—
ideas 'given without proof' and so new that the West re-
jected them and refused to believe in Madame Blavatsky's
initiation.

The two teachers' letters and her books form the most
solid base of belief in the Masters and, once they are read,
the legend ceases to be legend and becomes reality to any
impartial mind.

To this certitude, the book before us adds perhaps another. To gain the approval of scientific minds it is perhaps
a mistake to start out as a marvellous tale. But is this really wrong? Personally I do not think so, for I have noticed
that real life often has the outward appearance of a story.

For the reader, will this book trigger the beginning of a
life in which wisdom will replace the ordinary fluctuations
of passions? Less than one could believe. The transformation of our existence depends entirely on ourselves, and
no advice, from whatever source, can effectively change
us if the God who is in us, and is wiser than any Master,
has not spoken with his silent voice.

Furthermore, across from men who are too sceptical
there stand, equally disappointing and equally numerous,
men who are childishly credulous. Credulity loses its value
when it becomes superstition. People have wanted, in the
Himalayan Wise Ones, to see directors of humanity, kings
of the world, representatives of God on earth. Some even
describe in great detail a community in which Buddha, Pythagoras and Jesus Christ talked together with familiarity

under an age-old tree. I do not believe in the existence of this overly sublime community. What I do believe in seems to me more beautiful and more touching. The walls surrounding it are not protected from snow or wind. Food must be brought to it and clothes woven in it. It may be composed of men with infinitely broad knowledge and perfectly high moral standards, but one can discern, under the flowering of their power and their virtue, the root of their former human weakness. This is why I love them, as one loves older brothers, with a love all the greater because I know they have experienced my own mediocrity and have triumphed over it, have seen my own egoism and have known how to transform it into unselfishness.

To me, nothing seems more natural and plausible than that in Tibet there should be philosophers who, finding our vulgar life of pleasure distasteful, withdraw into the solitude of inaccessible hills where, by the culture of the mind, they acquire spiritual powers unknown to us. It is also plausible that they have managed to communicate with Wise Ones from other countries and to call them to their side. I imagine them sad to see their numbers grow so slowly. I imagine that, ill at ease with a greater sensitivity than ours, they are prisoners of their solitude. If they want to hold out their hand to us, they cannot do so. They must bring us their help by thought, and as our receptivity is almost non-existent, so is their influence, which can be exerted only on the best of us, those who are spiritually developed, that is to say very few. That which we call destiny or providence, a sequence of causes and effects, the strict law, is above all human will, above all Masters and all Gods. It restricts and leads everything that lives into

the unknown cycle of transformation. The Masters influence us and attract us to them only as far as our limited,
though ever-increasing, freedom permits—for freedom
grows with knowledge and moral development. They oc-
cupy the grade above that which we have attained and
prepare themselves for another state which is above ours
and about which we know nothing.

If, on our very earth, the Three Wise Ones of Agartha (to
be spoken of in this book and who are designated under the
name 'Great Lights') have an organisation unknown to us;
if they are grouped according to their intellectual and moral grade; if above their hierarchies are three Supreme Wise
Ones who lead them, then not only does this fail to offend
my reason but seems to me to be strictly logical. Above the
students in the process of perfection would be found three
men who have achieved perfection: that is, ones who would
have attained if not absolute perfection (which belongs to
the unknowable), at least whatever of it is attainable on
our planet. For the other Wise Ones they would represent
an image of the goal to be aimed at, the final degree on the
human scale. The revelations of Saint-Yves d'Alveydre in
'The Mission of India', despite their apparent unlikelihood,
would thus contain an element of truth.

For those concerned by these problems, here is an im-
mensely interesting fact: the mathematical method explained in this book allows communication with some of
these Wise Ones. It is true that we must not hold out too
much hope, but we must all the same see here a sign of
things to come: nothing happens by accident. Each act has
infinite consequences and the movement of even one grain
of sand echoes throughout the universe. The good deed

done by one of the authors of this book, a few years ago, has established a communication the effects of which will perhaps be very widespread. We are linked by a thread to this sort of silent vanguard, to these lovers of light, who nourish their pure love in such absolute silence that they seem to have no real existence. However it is probable that the communication will become more frequent and more intimate as we become worthy of it. The more sincerely we ask, the more helpful will be the replies. The closer to the Masters we become through our separation from selfishness, the more their voice will be heard by us, directly or without our knowledge.

The truth of the East, the wisdom kept by the unchanging watchmen of the Himalayan monasteries, has perhaps reached us and, however powerful our madness in not believing in it might be, and however great may be the blindness in which we immerse our sciences and our religions, it will eventually enlighten our minds, minds at last delivered from ignorance.

MAURICE MAGRE

THE MYSTERY OF SPIRITUAL LIFE

AN ESSAY BY JEAN MARQUÈS-RIVIÈRE

The title of this essay, as a preface for such a work, may seem strange. However, after having read '*Asia Mysteriosa*' one realises that the Method of Astral Force, which is the subject of the book, does in fact bring up the eternal problem of Spiritual Life and confirms the profound words 'the ways of the Spirit are innumerable'.

First of all, what is the value of this Oracle–Method? I must cite here my own direct personal testimony: it was made possible for me to consult notes on the subject taken over about 10 years; it was made possible for me to control the process of the Method; hundreds of replies made to various people I knew were shown to me; I myself asked many questions; I inserted Sanskrit and Tibetan words into these questions, not with any purpose in mind or out of pure curiosity (I wish this to be carefully noted) but to express an idea which seemed to me impossible to translate into any European language.

And here are my findings.

This method has a unique character; it has no connection with Cabalistic methods based on numbers and whose replies are on the 'yes or no' principle. I searched for similar methods in Asia and found none as full as this one. It seems that the mathematical tables we already have are but fragments of the one we are considering.

In Tibet there exist triangular tables, and I have knowledge of the texts of these, specifically; the numbers are combined in a particular order but the reply is always a version of 'yes' or 'no', or else in the form of insignificant sentences having a purely positive or negative character. There is nothing in these methods with the richness, the flexibility and the complexity of the 'Oracle' of Astral Force. I am in no doubt about its existence, for the replies obtained are often in contradiction to the thoughts of the enquirer and incomprehensible Sanskrit words are often given, words demanding much research. The important criterion is the result obtained; a tree is judged by its fruit.

Very clear general information is given out from the collection of replies: the Preface by Tek, received in its entirety through the method, is an admirable summary. After an unbiased study, I see no information in the West that comes close to its breadth of vision; we are used to schools, to small chapels and to nebulous and bookish metaphysics. The result is visible: such information has no effect on those who comment on it and thus the letter always kills the spirit. I sense in the Preface by Tek a completely practical vision of life and, above all, Spiritual Life. The BEING which communicates with us through the Method does not concern itself with words or sentences; HE SEES and expresses his vision in short, terse sentences of a sometimes superior inspiration; this transcendence enables him to be freed from space and time and this is why the Method predicts the future, remembers the past, and resonates with hearts. This is not all; because this unique logical solution must be acknowledged as marvellous; the Invisible Ones who direct know those who tackle the Method; the replies are proportional to the spiritual values of those who consult it, which is very important. Whatever the intellectual value of the enquirer, whatever his bookish science, if he is not sincere, humble of heart, worthy, and filled with FAITH, he can expect a reply which is abbreviated and, in a way, incomplete. If the enquirer approaches the Method with respect, the replies become profound, wise and indeed revelatory; eventually it is no longer the Oracle that sees the future and predicts Destiny but a Wise One who advises and helps the suffering man on life's path. The tone is strangely elevated: the replies thus become real, personal information which reminded me on many occasions of the wise words of the GURUS towards their CHELAS. This rule of spiritual adaptation is a general one which results in many misunderstandings; there is a sort of interference in the personal equation which, either on the way there or on the way back, 'colours' the ray connecting the enquirer to the BEINGS who are behind the Method (I do not know the mechanism, I give only a hypothesis). Disappointments have arisen from replies which have appeared inadequate; upon reflection they were logical, for they were addressed to those who deserved them to be exactly as they were; after having thought about this, I sometimes said to myself: 'I must admit that I asked the question out of sheer curiosity...'

There is another remark I must make before going any further. It seems to me that the information received is not in contradiction with that of Spiritualism. Nobody would be surprised that this troubles me; however, the reason for this seems serious to me, and it is as follows. Firstly, those who are interested in Spiritualism are much more numerous than is generally thought; next I must admit that in the West the only attempt at penetration into the mysteries of Life and Death has been done by Spiritualism. The leaders of spiritual groups themselves have told me that this attempt has been conducted by non-qualified people, which has resulted in errors, deflections and faulty interpretations erroneous to the point of crudeness. But in reality there is something else. It is easy to develop a theory on paper, but what does it mean in reality? The current regrettable failure of dogmas, of philosophical systems, is the most convincing proof of this. Spiritualism first approaches the problem directly; in itself, its method is good, for it is direct. The big danger, which has been mentioned by many researchers, is in the interpretation of the experiments. But the smallest sign, even contradictory, obtained through a visionary or a medium interests me much more than the many theories on the same subject. There is indeed enough material to construct, according to these signs, the main foundations of Spiritual Life. What is more, I must note that this material is obtained, in the East, in another way that I will call 'completely inward' but on which I will not elaborate here. These foundations are identical to those upon which rest the great human Traditions—and the harmony, here again, seems perfect between theurgist Science and experimental Spiritualism. Naturally it is only a question of *appearance* and it seems useless to me to dwell on the subject; it would be necessary to consider the problem of other sorts of appearance and that would be outside the scope of this essay.

Another important point must be made. It has been maintained many times that They who are behind the

Method are in Asia. This could be found surprising for
several reasons: first, why are they so far away? And in
admitting this, why use a Western form? Finally, who are
these mysterious BEINGS?

These three questions raise tremendous problems impossible to tackle in this essay. Here however is some information on the subject. The big question of the existence
of traditional Centres in Europe is still asked; however,
this seems to me to have been resolved a long time ago.
Since the seventeenth century, since the signature of the
Treaty of Westphalia (1648), which was of considerable
religious importance, it seems that the SIGN of the presence of any initiatic centre no longer exists in the West.
Little by little materialism has invaded the domains of
metaphysics, then philosophy, and finally religious matters. It is said, throughout a constant Tradition, that the
last representatives of these western Centres, whose outward appearance has often been given the name Rosicrucian, fled to the East at this time; it is also said that they
established themselves in Central Asia, leaving Europe
'for a time' to its destitution. Have times changed? Only
destiny can tell. It is worth noting that Swedenborg, who
was not in the least Eastern, affirms that one must look
for the 'Lost Word' among the Wise Ones of Tibet, and of
Tartary, and that Anne-Catherine Emmerich, whom I have
studied in particular, had very clear visions of the 'Mountain of Prophets', situated beyond Tibet, where all human
knowledge is conserved. These Centres are in Asia, therefore, for the purely material reason of the impossibility of
life in the West.

It is precisely this which explains the Western form of

the communications received. The Centre, Western in its essence and composition, retains in the East its qualities and its leanings; from the faraway East, it watches over the land of its brothers and thus a corner of the veil lifts. It is difficult to affirm anything at all and I leave it to the intuition of each individual to look further. I refer once more to the flight of the Rosicrucians, and will cite the marvellous visions of Anne-Catherine Emmerich ('Visions', 5th Edition, page 505): 'I also saw on another occasion that the body of Saint John did not remain on earth. I saw, between the West and the North, a place as radiant as a sun and I saw John there as an intermediary receiving something from on high to pass on to us. This place, although it seemed to me very high and completely inaccessible, was nonetheless part of the world...' Such a mystery, seen by such a Clairvoyant, seems wonderful to me. It clarifies things well, and more and more it seems true to me that 'at the end, little by little, all will be revealed'. A great unity of occult action thus shows through. I take pleasure in repeating that events are outside ourselves; more and more I attribute to them an almost absolute, and I would add even painful, objectivity. They impose themselves on us with such force which goes beyond us, with such power which crushes us, that only a God can act in such a way. FATUM, destiny, was created to explain the inexplicable: a word... We must look Truth in the eye, if that is possible. There is a magic chain clasping the world, a visionary told me: 'A HAND'... What are we? Nothing. Personal freedom, which nonetheless exists, is perhaps important *from an individual point of view*; from a cosmological point of view it is useless. Directives seem to be *given*; agents of a fantastic power seem to receive them and humans, like glove puppets, carry them out. It is a huge GAME, and this word which seems a witticism is found in many works of the TANTRAS, books of Asian esoteric science. However, one mysterious thing: there is conflict. There are angels of light and angels of darkness; we must, at a given moment, take sides: 'the lukewarm are abhorred'.

There is an even greater mystery, that which the Asian doctrines call THE MYSTERY OF REFLECTIONS. This is what the Wisdom of Egypt put on the Emerald tablet: 'As above, so below'. There is a strange harmony between the different levels of manifestation. Man has a sign that is found both on earth and in heaven. The Centre of transhuman power has indeed a reflection on earth; it is a constant tradition in Asia and this Centre (earthly? I do not know to what extent) is called, in Central Asia, Agartha. It also has other names that there is no need to include here. This Centre has as its mission, as its 'raison d'être', to lead the Earth's spiritual activities. To do this it uses *every possible means* and the following question arises: is this Method not one of these means? The tone of authority which it sometimes takes, the personal replies which change the lives of certain people I have been able to approach – are they not a SIGN? The three 'Little Lights' would be a sort of 'go-between', for it is obvious that everything must be given with 'order and measure' and that a glaring light must be filtered for too-feeble eyes. What is more, all this is strangely confirmed by very recent communications (1929) regarding the 'reconstruction of a group called 'Polaire' and whose esoteric statutes are in the process of being 'dictated' by the Method. The Centre in Asia wants a

Centre in Europe: and I am sure that with their fantastic power 'They' will obtain what they desire. The extraordinary phenomena taking place at the moment entirely confirms this for me.

I would now like to recall the words said to me *by someone who came from Asia*: 'Listen, listen… the Pure Doctrine and the Law (*tchoss*) are perpetually guarded: like a veil the Doctrine spreads and like a veil it folds; in times of trouble and adversity, the guardians put it away and It is kept thus, pure and without a blemish, in the immaculate snow…'.

THE ORACLE OF ASTRAL FORCE

*Mysterious Asia and the Oracle of Astral Force –
The 'Little Lights' – Father Julian – The Operator –
The 'Polaires' – The method of procedure of the
Oracle – The Astral Force – A hypothesis on
the psychological process of the Oracle.*

THE ORACLE OF ASTRAL FORCE

We have entitled these notes *Asia Mysteriosa* (Asia the Mysterious) because such was the wish of the 'Little Lights' with whom we are in communication, thanks to the Oracle of Astral Force, the strange arithmetical Method which we will be studying. The 'Little Lights' are the Wise Ones, the leaders of esoteric groups or monasteries around Agartha, this Initiatic Holy of Holies of the World, which traditions and legends situate precisely in the mysterious region of Asia that is the Himalaya.

It was, then, one of these 'Wise Ones' who gave the precious manuscript of the Method of Astral Force to its current keeper. The transmission of this troubling means of communication between the East and the West took place in 1908 in Bagnaia, a small village in the region of Viterbo,[1] where there lived a mysterious hermit whom the local people called Father Julian. The Hermit, who certainly wore the sign of the Rose and the Cross under his frock, disappeared from the village in 1909. For various reasons it was not until 1918 that it was asked, by way of the Method, where Father Julian could be found. The reply, which was particularly exact, should give us a thread of the fantastic web that we will try to unravel: 'His atonement is over. He has returned to his monastery in the Himalaya'.

Thus began many long years of study during which hundreds of communications were received and verified. These communications permitted us to realise that the Oracle of

[1]Province of Rome.

Astral Force did indeed constitute a link with the initiates
of groups around Agartha. But there is more: these communications gave us the certainty that this Method was a
foundation stone – real and tangible – laid by destiny on
the mysterious path of the occult. It happens that the time
is near when this stone will serve as a guide, a new Pole
Star, to those who feel lost in the darkness of the Earth.

When, about ten years ago, we were led to verify the Oracle of Astral Force – a divinatory Method enabling us to
obtain, by long arithmetical operations, strangely precise
replies – what urged us to study this procedure in depth
was hardly its divinatory character (which was particularly
troubling anyway) but the completely specific nature of
the communications obtained from it. These communications seemed, indeed, 'dictated' by mysterious entities and
sometimes designated facts, things and philosophies in a
particularly captivating way. We thought at first that these
replies were perhaps the result of a direct unconscious
clairvoyance, or not – but after a long verification of the
Method's *modus operandi*, we realised that as far as the
operator was concerned we had to rule out the development of a psychic phenomenon of this kind. Later, we had
to rule out also any empirical interpretation of signs or of
numbers[1] and, finally, any direct telepathic suggestion of

---

[1]We had already ruled out the possibility of the 'divinatory virtue of
numbers'. Given the process of the Method, this hypothesis was not even
something to consider (see note concerning the Cabala, page 67).

the answers. In fact, if these were obtained by clairvoyance or by suggestion, the absolute precision of calculations would not have been indispensable. On the contrary, however, just one error in the application of the rules of the Method or a simple calculation error was enough to obtain groups of numbers absolutely untranslatable into words. This observation thus seemed to constitute the irrefutable proof of the absence of any psychic phenomenon developing directly in the keeper of the Oracle of Astral Force.[1]

Before beginning our account of this Method, we will say that although our study and all our verifications were facilitated by the brotherly friendship which bound us to the keeper of the Method, on the other hand—and this weighed upon us like a wall of silence—it was very difficult for us to obtain consistent and really efficient work from him. When we bear in mind that the operator (which we will call him from now onwards) is obliged, because of his own personal occupations, to sacrifice sleeping time to the long hours necessary for the arithmetical development of a question, that he detests calculation, and that this task wearies him even more when the results he obtains from his work interest him in only a very relative way, we become aware of all the difficulties we have encountered during our research.

We have wanted to explain the frame of mind of our friend and the conditions in which he worked to give a

[1]See note, page 63, on this subject.

better understanding of the reason for any gaps that there
are in these notes. One must certainly not forget that although the operator may have given us the replies forming
the preface of Tek the Wise (which required nearly sixty
hours of calculations!), he sometimes made us wait weeks
and weeks before 'developing' a question which would
perhaps have enabled us to complete some particularly
interesting research. And so the time passed and we had
to make do with the 'material' that we had at our disposal
to comment on this strange means of communication with
the 'Chain of Initiation' in the Himalaya.

It is obvious that if our friend had been an enthusiast or
a mystery-seeker, the questions and answers would have
followed one another almost continually; but he is, alas,
neither the one nor the other and he has never wished,
at least until now, to give an important place on his Cur-
riculum Vitae to the strange method he possesses. There
is perhaps wisdom in this, and we should perhaps find in
this balance one of the reasons why this mysterious means
of communication was made known to him. Indeed, because of its importance and the possible results, it could
not have been entrusted to other than a fundamentally
well-balanced person who does not consider spiritual
Good as the only aim to achieve in this valley of tears and
of … *struggle for life*.*

We also wondered for many years why Father Julian, the
mysterious Hermit of Bagnaia, had given the Oracle of Astral Force to our friend, who was a distinct non-believer, if
not actively hostile to matters of the occult. This 'gesture'
of initiation, to be put in charge of such a formidable se-

---

*'Struggle for life' is in English in the original.

cret, may have been partly justified by the man's perfect psychological balance, and his faith in the given word, but the profound occult reason for the 'gesture' completely eluded us. It is only now, and only after having received certain communications,[1] that it is possible for us to presume that the 'reconstruction' of the Polaire Group and the coming of a Messenger from 'Asia Mysteriosa' seems to be the main esoteric reason for this unusual transmission of occult powers made by the Initiate to the humble passer-by marked by destiny.

The secret of the Method could not be revealed;[2] all that we have learnt about some of its rules, its arithmetical process and the psychic phenomena on which it is probably based is the fruit of our research, our observations and our studies. Each 'discovery', each new observation, led us to ask the operator a whole set of questions. He contented himself with answering 'yes' or 'no', depending on whether

[1] See page 111, "He Who Waits", the Supreme Spiritual Commander of the "Polaire" Group.

[2] A communication received in July of this year (1929) informed us that as soon as the "Polaire" Group (currently being formed) is reconstructed, this Method (The Oracle of Astral Force) should be communicated by its current keeper to a "Polaire" who will be designated later. Is not this transmission, which is probably coming soon, the strongest proof that our friend's psychic powers in no way come into play in the purely arithmetical development of the process which he possesses? (See Appendix, "The Polaires", on page 155).

our 'discovery' was accurate or erroneous. We admit that there could not have been a slower way of putting together, even roughly, a process as complicated as that of the Oracle of Astral Force, but it was the only means at our disposal of being able, as far as possible, to learn about its mechanism.

One day, tired of our research and our trial-and-error method, we decided to ask the Oracle:

'May I know the secret of the Method?'

The reply was clearly negative but very interesting:

REPLY: Your charge is too much [in English] ('Votre charge est trop lourde')

Ideal la locura [in Spanish] ('madness')

Impossibilité [in French; 'quite impossible']

Ben lo sapete [in Italian] ('You know full well')

This reply, though clearly negative, which we had rather expected (indicated by 'you know full well'), was nonetheless precious to us. Indeed, it was the first time that we had obtained a communication in four languages: English, Spanish, French and Italian, languages we know, and the first time that we were given the reply with idioms other than those with which the question had been asked. But, as precious as this communication could have been, it hardly gave us the key to the Oracle of Astral Force. So we returned to our slow research.

We will thus tell the reader all we know on the subject of the strange process of this method, or to put it better, all that we know up to now: perhaps someone more perspicacious or better informed than ourselves will be able to give us more details, which we would warmly welcome.

Modus operandi of the Method. – The question asked

must relate to something of the utmost importance to the interested party; it should be thought of very strongly by the interested party and written either in clear language or cryptically. It must include the petitioner's surname, Christian name and mother's Christian name (the petitioner being the person writing the question). The operator then transforms the letters and words of this question into numbers and groups of figures, to do which he conforms with the fixed rules of his arithmetical key.

Once this translation is done, the operator proceeds with:

1)   Calculations with the groups of figures obtained by the translation of the question;

2)   Calculations with the groups of numbers corresponding to the translation into figures and numbers of the surname, Christian name and mother's Christian name. It is here that the magic trinomial 3-6-9 comes into play, and it is with this that the operator embarks on very long operations;

3)   Calculations with all the results of these operations and the application of certain geometric combinations indicated in the Method.

The results of these final operations form the group of figures in which are found the numerical elements which, once translated into letters, will give perfectly-spelt words. However, it is to be noted that these words always come out as an incomprehensible 'puzzle', not yet having been put together to make a sensible sentence. To obtain the exact position of each word, the operator makes rapid calculations which indicate to him the number in sequence of each word, and he then has the reply as he should communicate it to the asker.

We have already said that the questions can be written either in clear language or cryptically but, in any case, the operator has no need to know the meaning of the question or the person writing it.

The number of words making up a question in no way relates to the number of words in the answer. To a very short question, a very long answer might be given, and *vice versa*. We shall have the opportunity to come back to this subject later.

The questions can be written in any language, but they must be translated into Italian because the numerical and alphabetical key the operator possesses does not enable him to translate with exactitude into figures questions asked in other languages.

Geometric figures or numerical symbols appear in some replies, but their meaning is always there to reinforce clarity in the text of the answers; this is with the exception, however, of communications addressed to those who know the symbolism of these figures or numbers. But, most important of all, to write the answer, the operator has never to interpret any sign or any number.

From what we have just set out, the interest that this strange Method generates will be understood, even before taking into account the divinatory value of its communications. Indeed, how can one obtain sensible and grammatically-perfect answers with simple calculations? What is the psychic phenomenon in play to obtain these answers? These are the questions we asked ourselves from the outset and which led us to delve into ancient and modern texts by Masters of the occult. The only practice that, in some of its forms – and in error, we admit now – seemed to us to have certain affinities with the Oracle of Astral Force, was Cabala.[1] This was why we decided to formulate the following question:

QUESTION: Is it a form of Cabala?

ANSWER: Remember that Astral Force is immense and must not be confused with Cabala. The questions must be asked while thinking without distraction and only for very serious things. Astral Force is all, which is as the Inconceivable wishes. If Ramples* was atrociously punished by the Chaldeans, it was because he rebelled against the Demfti Oracle of Astral Force.

To be honest, this reply, and many others, rather disconcerted us. What was understood by Astral Force? Was it

---

[1]Today we are perfectly well aware of the total and absolute difference between the Oracle of Astral Force and any form of divinatory Cabala. Indeed, whatever the apparent, and deliberate, complication of Cabalistic divinatory methods, they are all based on 'yes' and 'no', the Urim and Thumim of Israeli Priests. From the most simple to the most complicated, from the *Ars Magna* of Ramon Lulle to the divinatory fantasies of Cabalistic Jews of the Middle Ages, all are merely games of heads or tails. There are some which can give 284 different replies in Latin (the favourable lines alternating with the unfavourable); there are some which reply to questions asked in any language or 'jargon', but the translation of the question into figures and the long calculations necessary to obtain the reply are only a way of giving importance to the method, to lend it a mysterious air which disappears as soon as the process used is dissected. What is more, the replies are always the same and all written in the same language. Should these divinatory methods be considered a mystification? We do not think so; it is very possible that certain Cabalistic applications are effective for all strictly personal questions, to which an affirmative or negative reply is sufficient.

*I have sought in vain for the identity of Ramples—editor.

Universal Force, the magic universal agent designated by
the occultists of all time under so many different names?
Was not the Force defined by Hermes Trismegistus in the
ninth proposition of his Emerald Tablet as: 'the Force,
strong with all forces, for it will overcome all things subtle
and penetrate all things solid'?* What part did the Egyptians Ramples and Demfti play in this answer? We dealt
later with this last question[1] but immediately formulated
the following question:

QUESTION: What is Astral Force?

*ANSWER: Radiance. Destiny. Balance. If you
need a preface for what you are writing, ask for it,
calling upon Tek the Wise.*

This superbly synthesising definition of Astral Force[2]
confirmed our hypothesis and gave us a glimpse of elements of the probable psychic phenomenon playing a part
in the writing of the question and the answer.[3]

It would be, in fact, at the moment the question is strongly
thought of, without distraction, that contact would be made,

[1]See the analysis of the Chaldean indication, page 123.

[2]Definition adapted to our plan (the Spirit = Radiance; Destiny = the
Astral; Balance = the Physical Body).

[3]Properly to understand this definition of Astral Force, we will recall that all esoteric traditions recognise a Universal Force, the cause
of all the manifestations and differentiations of the Cosmos. It divides
and sub-divides into a quantity of different manifestations and the sonic,
luminous, Hertzian, psychic, etc., vibrations would be created by it. It
is these 'psychic vibrations' (telepathic waves, magnetic, etc.) that per-

by means of 'telepathic waves', between the questioner and our Correspondents. Becoming informed of the questioner's thought, they mentally impose upon him, by the same method, the precise terms of the written question. This question would thus be whispered in such a way that the operator, making the calculations indicated by the Method, would obtain the reply desired by our mysterious Correspondents.

To explain our idea better we will place ourselves on essentially mathematical ground – simplifying, of course, the very complicated rules of the Method.

Let us suppose, then, that the manuscript's fixed rules indicate to the operator the following calculations:

1)   Transform into numbers and figures the letters and words of the question, following the arithmetical key.

2)   Multiply the groups of figures obtained by this transformation by 10 and multiply the product by 3.

3)   Transform the result of this last operation into letters and words. This will constitute the reply.

Now, let us assume that the reply the Initiate wishes to give, transformed into figures, corresponds to the number 600. To put forward the question-problem, one has only to do the same calculations as the operator, but in reverse order and with opposite signs:

$$600 : 3 = 200 \qquad 200 : 10 = 20$$

---

mit, under special conditions, the reception or transmission of psychic messages (unconscious phenomenon to the normal being – conscience to the hypersensitive psychic). This phenomenon of thought transmission (unconscious or willed) allows a better understanding of the psychic mechanism of the Oracle of Astral Force.

*The ninth proposition of the Emerald Tablet is a unifying one, variously translated, but a rendition from the Arabic gives: 'The greatest power overcomes everything that is subtle and it penetrates all that is coarse'.

The number 20, transformed into letters and words, will constitute the question 'whispered' mentally by the Initiate to the questioner.

The operator, once in possession of this question, translates it into figures and, given that his numerical key is the same as that used by the Initiate, will inevitably obtain the number 20. Consequently, on applying the rules to his Method, he will get:

$$20 \times 10 = 200 \qquad 200 \times 3 = 600$$

—that is to say, the number constituting the reply (in reverse order, we repeat) dictated by the Initiate.

It could be argued that the operator takes hours to 'obtain' this reply, while the reverse calculations could be done almost instantaneously by the Initiates. To this we will reply that an Inaudi,* to do the same calculations, would take a few minutes. We can thus recognise that the Initiates – gifted with supernormal psychic means, do not forget – can reply at the speed of thought. However, we do not know in which way they make these calculations or if they use the same arithmetical procedures as the operator.

The reply defining Astral Force gives us perhaps the key to the psychic phenomenon of the process of the Method, and it confirms above all – and indisputably – that the Oracle of Astral Force really was a method of communication with mysterious Initiates. So who was Tek the Wise? Why was he to dictate a preface for what we were to decide to write just four years later?

*Jacques Inaudi (1867–1950) was an Italian calculating prodigy.

TEK THE WISE

Tek the Wise – his Preface – Humility – Yang
and Yin – Destiny – Evolution – the Worlds – the Spark
– Involution – Spiritual Phenomena – Death –
the Return to the Inconceivable

TEK THE WISE

Tek?– a distinctly intentional phonic 'con-formation' of the Tibetan word 'Theg', which is pronounced almost exactly as our Correspondents 'dictated' it : Tegk (the H being a purely phonic accessory to indicate that the T is hard).

It was this Wise One, whose initiatic importance we will see later, who gave us the longest communication we had ever received: his Preface.

This Preface, despite its apparent strangeness, embraces in its 480 words the most tremendous problems man has ever faced, lost and powerless as he is: destiny, the beyond, the phenomenon of involution, unknown worlds…

Over all of this philosophy there hovers a detachment from worldly things, so that the return to the Ineffable takes place without passing through the tortuous paths of future Lives…

Who is Tek the Wise? The translation of his name seems to answer this. He is the 'Method', the 'Way', 'He Who Helps', 'He Who Raises Up', 'He Who Endures'… Indeed 'They' told us that this Wise One bore one of the most overwhelming burdens ever given to an incarnate being to bear…[1]

[1]According to the occult investigations conducted in collaboration with Madame Jeanne Canudo and Mademoiselle Renée Remande, I can state that Tek the Wise is an initiate following for centuries a clear mission: the transmutation of the human mass's sentimental devotion into intuitive mysticism. This will of redemption attaches him to the mass of humanity and Dante would have rightly placed him in one of the circles of Purgatory. For example, Tek the Wise belongs to the occult Spiritualist trend, powerful but dubious, which has given rise to and still supports the 'Army of Salvation'. Previously Tek the Wise supported another Spiritualist trend,

Like Father Julian, the Hermit, he supports and expiates that he may help, and to indicate the Way.

Here is his preface:[1]

'Man thinks he knows, and knows nothing. When he begins to know, to see the true light, then such is destiny that he must leave the world of incarnates, for spirit and matter are incompatible.

'O troubled being who will read this book, remember that true power lies in humility and the finest work is to help those who have fallen. At the moment of committing a bad action, try to avoid it, for we must account for everything.[2] The first Pharaoh, who was nevertheless a Son of the Sun,[3] lost his superior spirituality for having neglected an essential element of Justice.[4]

'Yang and Yin,[5] in their eternal struggle, are the two Forces which settle everything. Man is born with his

[1]This preface is composed of seven communications and 480 words (in Italian).

[2]Here, the accounting is both spiritual (indicated in the communication by a triangle) and material (indicated by a square).

[3]Tek the Wise seems to confirm the 'legend' that the first Pharaoh was an Atlantean (son of the Sun).

[4]Justice is the stabilising power *par excellence*. It is the highest expression of spirituality, for nothing can be good if it is not just.

[5]In Chinese philosophy – Yang: Heat, Light, the Sky, the Male Principle. Ying: Cold, Shadow, the Earth, the Female Principle (negative). In the Temple of the Sky in Peking, Yang is represented by a white stone and Ying by a black stone.

equally powerful and equally dubious, that of the 'Whirling Dervishes'. His wish is to clarify this flood of unintelligent mysticism. An epithet applied to him characterises him very well: 'The Madman's Wise Man' (striving towards transmuting mystical folly). A Titanic task! A work of sacrifice also, for we know that the Universal Law of Cause links the Redemptor on the Cross with his Action for the millions of years over which this action bore fruit (note by M.Vivian du Mas.)

Destiny already mapped out, for this is how it should be, but he is arbitrator to choose between Yang and Yin. Only in very special cases, a being can change the course of another existence, and this is called a 'double reflection' mission. This mission allows us to have the certitude of passing by evolution to a Superior World.[1] Destiny is the fruit of a previous life lived in another World in circumstances which men cannot understand. The worlds which must be travelled in countless existences are numberless, but what is certain is that no return is made to the same world.

'By Divine Law, all is settled in such a way that the Spark* of a materially dead being comes, attracted as if by a magnet, into a body being born in another world. This world can even be billions of your miles away from Earth. There are Sparks which stay for centuries without finding the magnet that attracts them to another world. This is because of a special need for contemplation and an attachment to the Astral to learn what they needed to learn in their lifetime – and thus accomplish their evolution so as to be ready for attraction. Some of these phenomena that you consider spiritual phenomena are due to these Sparks within the astral, which – at times – take a lively role in earthly matter, for good or for ill, for they are still dominated by human sentiments.[2] May the Inconceivable remember them!

[1]Evolution: passage from one level (or world) to a superior level (or world).

[2]We find here the Legions of Angels and Demons, of Prophets and Visionaries.

*Apparently, the essential individual being, the seed atom of the individual.

'The most beautiful reward (that is to say the breath of destiny which extinguishes the flame of material existence) is accepted by many with terror. This proves that such minds are not evolved minds. That which we call death is but life in always-superior conditions, for the painful ordeal of existence on earth comes to an end and this is a step towards better existences.

'The deaths of children are special cases, for young ones do not understand life and suffer nothing of it. We are talking about evolved Sparks, destined to bring suffering among those nearest them, in order to prepare them for evolution.[1] There are also cases in which the profound turmoil of attraction is enough to make these sparks ready to be called to a new existence in other worlds.[2]

'O poor being, why torture your existence for ever bigger dreams and ambitions? Why all of this? You must always die to be reborn and be reborn to die, until the moment when you are absorbed into the Inconceivable.[3] In the presence of this immense truth your day is worth the same as theirs who are more powerful or less powerful than yourself, for you must always die to be reborn and be reborn to die...'[4]

It is in no way our intention to comment on the Preface

[1]Evolution through pain. It is in the trial of pain that men transform themselves and evolve towards a superior spirituality.

[2]It is as if these sparks were insufficiently retained in their physical receptacle, the human body.

[3]The return to God. This is the Paradise of various religions, while Purgatory would correspond to survival in other worlds.

[4]This sentence, well worthy of the philosophy of those who have no material connections, indicates that our struggles for life here below are useless, and it would be preferable to orientate all our efforts towards spiritual

of Tek the Wise. It reflects the wisdom of Those who have no material attachments: Tibetan lamas or Christian monks of an unknown solitary retreat. This dense philosophical account, whether it sinks into the night of centuries or flies high and far towards the supreme truth, may appear strange, bizarre and uneven in the power of its flight... But if one reflects, if one meditates, if one raises oneself above the literal sense of the words and dogmas, one will see that it illuminates everything with a burning splendour beyond what man's 'eyes of flesh' can conceive.

Furthermore, this Preface is a good reflection of the philosophy which comes from the communications that we have received, all having the same end: spiritual elevation. Everything in it indicates that the Way is the renunciation of worldly things, and that real power is humility in front of That ... the utter immensity of which our mind cannot comprehend.

We will not say, however, that the 'letter' is always the same: there are, it is said, 22 pagodas in Agartha. Is this the number of Ways which lead to the Light? Is this the number of initiatic languages – teaching, all of them, the Word? We do not know. But from all of these communications comes the incredible impression of finding ourselves in the presence of a Centre which has collected all the Traditions of the World... And one thus has the feeling that the clairvoyance of Catherine Emmerich, the 'illuminism' of Saint-Yves d'Alveydre, and the teachings of the Lamas and the Tibetan gurus, and of the Brahmins and the Hindu yogis, are not dreams.

---

refinement; whereas the return to God is by our 'always greater' dreams and ambitions and the struggles they inevitably create. We prepare for ourselves a long series of existences before attaining the indefinable level.

SYMBOLISM AND PHILOSOPHY

The Luminous Hierarchies – Light and Darkness –
The Missions – Destiny and Free Will – Mohammed –
The Dates – Illnesses and Remedies – The Acputus

SYMBOLISM AND PHILOSOPHY

Our Correspondents' communications[1] often had an oracular style : ' Men who think they know, but know nothing'. 'He will enter into oblivion, for he will have to atone for the sin which nothing can erase'. 'The fatal Comet, which will plunge humanity into a limitless pain, is still far away'[2]

Sometimes the communications appear, at first glance, almost anodyne, but once checked, and the facts tested, one realises that, point by point, what seemed generic becomes precise and is seen in its true light. The replies seem to be dictated by various entities, with the exception of those signed 'Julian' and those belonging to the same particular group of questions. They are generally written in a rather archaic, though always perfect, Italian, despite the telegraphic form used. In certain cases one would say they were dictated by a foreigner with a perfect knowledge of Italian spelling but conserving the sentence structure of his own language.

The symbolic leitmotif of the communications is based

[1]For reasons that are easily understood, we were obliged to select these communications from among those of a not too personal nature.

[2]The Comet here indicated War. Note that in the Sibylline Oracles war is always attributed to the influence of a Comet.

on Light, on the Sun.[1] This is the Sun of the Initiates, that which has been defined by Orpheus as follows: 'The Sun which I evoke above your heads, and which will shine in your souls, is not the sun of mortal beings, it is the pure light of Dionysus, the great Sun of the Initiates'.

It is for this reason that the Inconceivable,[2] the Almighty, the Most High, is often called 'the Greatest Light'; that Christ, the Sun God of Christian Cabalists, is defined as 'Light without equal'; and that Socrates and Buddha are 'Great Lights'. After these, there are the Three Wise Ones – with whom we are in direct communication – who hold the name of 'Little Lights', while the sages of the other initiatic groups are referred to in the same manner, but 'coloured in': the Radiant Light Elos, the Green Light, the Yellow Gold Light, Sublime Irridescence, etc, etc.

However, beside the Light there are the Shadows, the obscure Forces, the harmful Forces. These Forces are also called 'Groups of Negative Light': obscure Powers, Powers without Light, which seem to culminate in the '3 without 3',[3] that is to say the inversed Triangle, the black Triangle

[1]On this subject we must note the solar role attributed to arithmetic (visionary reason) by the Cathars. The scientific system of these Initiates was based on the doctrine of correspondence, and arithmetic actually corresponds to the Sun.

[2]The Inconceivable appears, in the replies, as the great God and inexorable upholder of the law of Israel: 'Your family was partially destroyed on a day when destiny, by the will of the Inconceivable, unleashed adversity and destruction'. Note that the different denominations of the Inconceivable are generally accompanied by one, two or three triangles whose angles are placed in three small circles (the 'YOD' character of celestial writing).

[3]The '3 without 3' is the inversed Triangle which always has the same numeric value attributed symbolically to the Triangle (i.e., 3) but in which cannot be written the number 3, the Cabalistic symbol of the spir-

of the Cabalists. And the eternal struggle between Good and Evil, in certain communications, takes on a really agonising scale.

We continued with our work on the Method of Astral Force :

*QUESTION: What must I do to keep it?**

REPLY: Your mission is vast, but you must accomplish it; evil forces are working against the Method. Try to attract it into your magnetic circle and, if you will it, you will succeed. Death is suffering and expects this of you. Remember: Qui sine peccato est vestrum primus mittat lapidem.†

(Here the words of the 'Light without equal' could not find, in their infinite mercy, a better adaptation to the question's subject.)

QUESTION: Why have you not helped us?

REPLY: Because from the very beginning of your work you have been surrounded by evil forces, thus moving the Little Lights[1] away from you.

QUESTION: What are the evil forces surrounding us?

REPLY: Groups of negative light. Ambitious, dark forces.

This was our work on the Method of Astral Force. We were discouraged, even frightened, by the difficulties we

[1]Reminder: The 'Little Lights' are the Wise Ones.

*'Pour la sauver'—it is unclear what the context is.

†'He that is without sin among you, let him first cast a stone at her'. John 8 : 7

_____

itual plane. The inversed Triangle is the ideogram of darkness, specifically: the Devil, and the negation of Spirituality.

found on our path. We had the feeling that the mysterious thread connecting us to 'Those' over there had broken. We were not wrong.

These communications were followed, shortly afterwards, by another of a similar nature:

QUESTION: May we begin (our publication)?

REPLY: Do not begin until the November Moon, for at the moment you are surrounded by dark forces (reply intended for the author).

Why did the Powers of Light not put to flight the evil forces, the groups of negative light, the dark forces? Was it impossible for them to intervene in the struggles created by karmic necessities? This mysterious problem of unknown forces surrounding us, watching us, which desired to push us towards darkness, completely eluded our poor human logic. We remain with the hallucinatory feeling of being surrounded by a demonic Sabbath, forever ready to drag us towards the abyss.

All of the answers confirm free will for part of life's happenings; for the remaining part, it is fatality, destiny, the inexorability of events that are in preparation and which nothing can erase or modify. These events, according to the Preface of Tek the Wise, are inescapably linked to the life of the human being, for he has prepared them during his previous life, lived on another 'planet', on another plane. It is by the law of karma[1] that our path, at birth, is

[1]Here we are using the word karma in the Theosophical sense. Karma:

traced, inexorably traced; and free will exists only as a preparation for karma of a new life 'on another Planet, on another plane'.

We will say that all 'fatal' events come from the karmic net we have woven in our former life, and the things over which we exert complete free will prepare the karma of the next life. It is as if, in the immutable path of destiny, there were for each life a dark side and a light side. It is in choosing sometimes one and sometimes the other that we create the 'causes' of future 'effects'.

Here is a good example of a communication referring to free will :

QUESTION: Will I win? (This refers to a very important court case.)

REPLY: That depends on you. You will win if you learn to pay attention to small details. It is often things that seem small and insignificant which determine big things.

And a communication referring to fatal inexorability:

QUESTION: Must I choose the route you know?

REPLY: You have not to choose. Your route is marked by the Force nothing can stop. Raise your spirit and, at the end of the long road, you will find the light you are looking for.

---

consequences of cause and effect, a chain joining all actions to their results. In accordance with the Law of Karma, man is born under fatal influences which affect him and his life according to decisions generated in his previous lives. (Rhéa Dictionary, Paris 1921)

Our correspondents do not reply to 'immoral' questions
(and by immorality we do not mean what is based on the
hypocrisy of prejudices and social conventions), but they
are compassionate judges of, and advisors on, our human
woes, though they never forget to remind us of the true
aim in life: 'The Great Prophet of the Eternal Black Stone
said:[1] "Men, you who rest in your women's arms, do not
forget that this life is but the preparation for the true life".'
What is more, they are rich in advice when it comes to
things of real interest to the questioner:

QUESTION: *What will the solution be?*

REPLY: *Why did you let your propitious moment
pass? You will now have to resolve the problem by the
second combination.*

QUESTION: *Is there a possibility of a second combination? With what result?*

REPLY: *For you the result will be like a web of*

---

[1]The Great Prophet of the Eternal Black Stone: Mohammed. The Black
Stone is found in the Qaaba of Mecca. This Stone, according to Arab
authors, was originally a white hyacinth. When Abraham and Ishmael
built the Temple, Gabriel brought it to them. Following this, an impure
woman having touched it, it lost its brilliance and turned black. 'Victors
over their enemies, the Quraishites dreamed of erecting a monument to
their glory. The Qaaba, this antique sanctuary they were guarding, could
not contain the numerous Tribes in its narrow enclosure. They wanted to
widen it. The temple was demolished and rebuilt where the Black Stone
should have been laid. They all wanted to have the honour of laying it
in its place. After much debate, it was agreed to leave the decision to
the first one to enter the Temple. Chance led Mohammed there. He was
chosen as judge. He decided that they should place the Black Stone on a
long carpet, each extremity of which would be held by a man from each
of the Tribes, and that they would all lift it together. Once it had been sufficiently raised, Mohammed took it in his hands and put it in its place.'
('Abridged Life of Mohammed' by M.Savary, Garnier Brothers, Paris)

thorns. Avoid such a combination.

QUESTION: Advise me – what must I do?

REPLY: A maxim of the Great Warrior of Medina[1] will be useful and will help you: 'Be quiet – meditate profoundly – speak and act at the right moment'.[2]

However, our correspondents may be helpful and compassionate towards our human worries, but they hardly seemed disposed to being bothered in the case of simple curiosity. An occultist of Rome,[3] wishing to learn the *modus operandi* of the Method, wrote a long question to find out the first word of the fifth page of the fifth book in a nearby drawer. The reply, 'developed' in his presence, was very simple: 'Why do you ask that?', thus indicating that this sort of question was absolutely useless.

The dates are often indicated in relation to astral movement: 'She will return when Titania* and Venus form a triangle with Uranus' – 'Soon, that is when the northern constellations Bootes and the Dragon form an arc'. In any case, for some time, our correspondents, as if realising the

---

[1]The Great Warrior of Medina: Mohammed, whose tomb is, in fact, in Medina. This town was also called Medinet en-Nébi: Town of the Prophet.

[2]This reply, like many other transcripts in these notes, seems insignificant, but it is not. In this case, on the contrary, it afforded the questioner with a precious piece of advice.

[3]J. Evola, author of 'Magic Idealism', 'The Tantras', etc.

*A Moon of Uranus.

difficulties presented for us by this astronomical research, gave us precise dates by counting generally in 'moons' (months), in 'sunrises' (days) or according to our calendar.

QUESTION: May I conclude?
REPLY: Before concluding, wait until the end of the first month of your year.[1]

QUESTION: What should I expect?
REPLY: The inevitable. For 200 sunrises you will be able to change nothing. Illusion is the sweet poison of the soul.

QUESTION: How much longer before something disappears?
REPLY: On the 25th of December – understand this well – something will disappear.

QUESTION: Will it be favourable?
REPLY: Three things are missing, then it will be favourable. Ask again after thirteen sunrises.

QUESTION: Please indicate to me if I may hope for an immediate settlement of the matter X.
REPLY: You will have the reply for the settlement of X in eight sunrises, the favourable time for this.
QUESTION: Father Julian, advise me.
REPLY: Dear Son, for many, many moons I can do nothing for you, nor advise you.

---

[1]The first month of our year: January.

The chemical and medical terms seem strange, but some diagnoses were surprisingly precise:

QUESTION: Is my pain serious?
REPLY: Your pain could become serious if you do not try to change it. Changing it means taking care of yourself and raising your spirit to beautiful things in order to acquire the serenity that is Life. The influence of Neptune could do you much good. So, Sea... Sea and Sea. Iodine has a density, in its solid state, of 4.95 and in its gaseous state of 8.716. So it is the only cure that will always suit your case.

The following communications refer to a group of questions concerning the search for a remedy for malaria (from an old 17th Century recipe)

QUESTION: Tell me if my remedy is effective.
REPLY: Insufficient – but in certain cases it could heal.
QUESTION: Must I add gentian?
REPLY: Gentian is of little significance. For the remedy to be effective you must soak Acputus roots under lunar influence.

The questioner searched everywhere, among old herbal recipes, in botanical dictionaries, without finding the word 'Acputus'. He therefore asked another question.

QUESTION: Please tell me where I may find Acputus roots.

REPLY: Acputus does not grow in Europe. You will find what you are looking for in the grape, but in a very small quantity, insufficient to heal.

QUESTION: To treat suffering humanity, tell me where to find Acputus or how to obtain it, or the European herb that can effectively replace it.

REPLY: Only those with such a mission can treat suffering humanity. Bodily illness: true Light of the Soul* – such was the faith and the Great Light of Socrates. There exists no plant to replace Acputus. There is only a very small quantity in the grape.

QUESTION: Please indicate a method of clarifying my elixir (still referring to the same remedy).

REPLY: Take care of the filtering process, then two minus two.

(Cabalistically, two signifies imperfection, 2 minus 2 means: imperfection disappears.)

The questioner, hardly satisfied with the replies concerning Acputus (offended in his 'unworthiness' to treat suffering humanity) asked another question.

QUESTION: Why do you not want to tell me where Acputus is found?

REPLY: Why insist when we cannot…(reply).

This was a reply indicating the discipline of Initiates and which the communications we now transcribe will help to clarify.

QUESTION: Please tell me if there exists a remedy

---

*That is, things that seem ill from this side of life may be good from the other side of life.

*for my brother's tubercular laryngitis and if he can
recover.*

*REPLY: All remedies exist in nature, but the Incon-
ceivable does not allow egotistical humanity to find
them. Where the white flowers of snow[1] are born, he
will be able to improve his condition.[2]*

QUESTION: Please tell me if X will recover.

*REPLY: For certain wounds the Inconceivable
sends to Humanity for atonement, there are no
remedies. To relieve his suffering a little, Humanity
should try to distance the evil influences surrounding
it* (by prayer).

This concerned a female cancer sufferer – a very serious condition.

The outcome of all these communications is:

1) That all remedies exist in nature.

2) That the Inconceivable does not allow them all to be
found.

3) That only those with a mission to do so can discover
them.

Under these conditions, it not seem to us that the replies concerning Acputus have to be considered as a les-
son for the questioner, who was acting in complete good
faith, and even less as an act of mystification. Actually
there is, in these communications, an indication which
could be precious, namely that in the grape there is, in

[1]This is the Edelweiss.

[2]This diagnosis was confirmed – indeed as were many others – by
the eminent Professor G.P.M. Inghilleri of the University of Rome. He
declared that it would be necessary to transport the sufferer to a high
mountain Sanatorium to try to prolong his life.

a very small quantity, a remedy for one of the scourges of
humanity: malaria.[1]

THE THREE SUPREME WISE ONES

The Three Wise Ones – The Dazzling Astral Force – The
Tradition of the Three Wise Ones – The Magic Numbers
– Agartha and its Traditions – The Three Wise Men –
Mohammed and Agartha – The 'Little Lights' – The King
of the World – The Inconceivable – The 'Little Light
Julian' – The Three Supreme Wise Ones and Agartha –
The Guardians of the Mystery of Life and Death – The
Babylonian Method of Astral Force – Agartha and the
History of the World.

THE THREE SUPREME WISE ONES

Having tried one day to develop a question written in German, the Operator obtained in reply only geometric signs with no significance for us.

QUESTION: What is the meaning of this reply? (We assumed that the Cabalistic interpretation of the signs completely escaped us.)

REPLY: No meaning. The key to the Astral Force you are addressing is for the Italian language. It can reply in other languages, but only in special cases. Verification will always be required. Only the Three Wise Ones △ △ △ can reply in all languages, including the most ancient.

So who were these Three Wise Ones whose numerical symbols, written in the three triangles, were the same as those of the Oracle–Method?

A second communication, obtained a few days later, confirmed this symbolism, and this designation:

'The Dazzling Astral Force, which you cannot conceive, is found in the Monastery of the Three Wise Ones △ △ △ . The indication concerning the weak Astral Force which you know is found in Brahmaputra[1] in the hands of the old King.[2] Ask for what you are seeking.'[3]

[1]Brahmaputra: old sanctuary on the river of the same name.

[2]King: symbolic name of Chinese origin. There are numerous interpretations of this name.

[3]So we asked: *'I wish to know in which European books the Astral Force is mentioned as a divinatory method.'* REPLY: *'In none. The*

The eminent occultist Professor Reghini, director of the review of initiatic studies, *Ignis*, to whom we communicated these two replies, wrote us the following note: 'It seems to me that there exists a certain connection between these communications and what is written by Saint-Yves d'Alveydre and Ferdynand Ossendowski on the subject of the Three Wise Ones. Consider what Saint-Yves d'Alveydre wrote, in his posthumous book, about the subterranean world of Agartha and the King of the World, *The Mission of India* (1910),[1] and that written by Mr Ossendowski on the same subject in his now famous book *Beasts, Men and Gods* (1924). They both put three Wise Ones at the head of Agartha. According to Saint-Yves, the Supreme Chief holds the title of Brahâtmâ (support of souls in the spirit of God) and his two assistants are Mahâtmâ, who represents the universal soul, and Mahânga, symbol of all material organisations in the Cosmos. Ossendowski, whose sources of information are Mongolian (while those of Saint-Yves are Hindu) wrote: Brahytma, Mahytma and Mahynga: Brahytma, the King of the World, can speak with God, and of his two assistants Mahytma is he who knows future events and Mahynga he who directs the causes of these events. It is obvious that one could very easily develop Cabalistic correspondences between the symbols of the Three Wise Ones, those of the King of the World and of his two assistants, and put into contact,

---

[1]Dorbon-Aîné, Paris

only European book was stolen by a French soldier in Moscow.'
   Would this be a book taken to Moscow by Genghis Khan, 'stolen' by him during one of his forays into North India and translated into a European language?

symbolically, Brahâtma with the 3, Mahâtmâ with the 6 and Mahânga with the 9.'[1]

Whether from the Wise Ones of Agartha or the King of the World and his two assistants, our communications thus came to confirm a tradition as old as the world, that of the Three Wise Ones.

[1]These numbers constitute the symbol of the Oracle-Method of Astral Force and that of the Three Supreme Wise Ones (and probably also that of Agartha). They correspond to three Cabalistic Worlds: Spiritual –3-, Astral –6-, Physical –9-. They form the sacred Triad of Pythagoras: simple (3), level or square (6), solid or cubic (9); a very clear indication of a common initiatic origin is the fact that these 'magic' numbers are also found in numerous Hindu traditions, in the Chaldean tradition, in the Mantras (the 9 Triangles intertwined by groups of 3 or the 3 Triangles of which two are intertwined as in the 'Seal of Solomon', and the third written in the middle hexagon), in the Koran, in the offering of the Sibylline Books by the Sybille Cumaine to Tarquin the Superb, in Dante's 'Divine Comedy', in the symbolism of the Rosicrucians, etc. They also correspond to the 7 planets and the 2 Luminaries.* To resume: they constitute the symbolism of all initiations, assuming evolution and involution, ascension and descent, and the 3 fundamental principles of the macrocosm and microcosm.

It is to be noted that these numbers also correspond to the political and religious organisation of Tibet: '...I learnt the secret links between the philosophic Doctrine and political constitution of Tibet. The 3 aspects of Universal Science (Theurgist Science, Spiritual Science and Physical and Material Science) are represented by the Three Centres of Force which dominate Tibet with their overwhelming splendour and their formidable power. The Tashi-Lama, who commands Gods and Demons, who lights the Flames of Gold before the Statues of Ancestors by its magic power alone; the Dalai Lama which reflects pure spirituality, the quiet and luminous metaphysic of Asia; and the Bogdo Khan, the Prince of North Mongolia, powerful war influence, overseeing the Military and secret Societies of all Asia.' (The Tashi Lama (3), the Dalai Lama (6), the Bogdo Khan (9))† – Jean Marquès Rivière: *In the Shadow of Tibetan Monasteries.*

*That is, the Sun and Moon.

†The Tashi Lama is the former European name for the Panchen Lama, while Bogdo Kahn is the Bogdo Lama, the Emperor of Mongolia.

Indeed, we saw them as appearing under various denominations, in almost all religious traditions. They are the Three Wise Ones of Atlantis, the Three Druids who created the Heavens and the Gods, the Three Old Ones who gathered the word of Brahma, the Three Wise Ones who bowed down before the cradle of Krishna, the Three Wise Men who laid offerings of Incense, Gold and Myrrh[1] at the feet of the Divine Child, the Three White Tibetan Gods Gouban, Zourghan and Bourkhan and, finally, they are Brahâtma, Mahâtmâ and Mahânga of Saint-Yves d'Alveydre's Hindu tradition, and Brahytma, Mahytma and Mahynga of Ossendowski's Mongol legend.

However this tradition, which dominates or accompanies the great spiritual demonstrations, is followed by another that is equally important, that of an initiation centre, a mysterious 'monastery' where all Initiations and all white traditions come together…

In the marvellous synthesis called *The King of the World*, by René Guénon, we find this mysterious Centre described as follows: 'From all the testimonies which agree, a conclusion emerges very clearly: the affirmation that there exists a "Holy Land", a spiritual Centre to

---

[1]The tradition of the Catholic Church on the subject of this offering says that the Incense was offered to God, the Gold to the King and the Myrrh to Man. It is easy to see, in this tradition, the correspondence of the Three Worlds with the numbers 3-6-9. See pp. 103–4: the esoteric tradition concerning the Three Wise Men explained in *The King of the World* by Mr. Guénon (published by Bosse, Paris).

which all other Centres are subordinate. The "Holy Land" is also the "Land of the Blessed", the "Land of the Living", the "Land of Immortality": all of these expressions are equivalent, and we must also add that of the "Pure Land" which Plato applied specifically to the "dwelling place of the Blessed". This dwelling place is usually situated in an "invisible world" but, if we want to understand it, we must not forget that it is the same as "spiritual hierarchies" also mentioned by all traditions and which represent in reality the degrees of initiation.

'In the current period of our earthly cycle, that is to say in the Kali Yuga, this "Holy Land", defended by "Guardians" who hide it from the eyes of the profane even while they maintain certain external connections, is indeed invisible and inaccessible, but only to those who do not have the necessary qualifications to penetrate it. Should its location in a specific region now be regarded as literally real or merely as symbolic, or is it both of these at once? In answer to this question we would simply say that to us, as with all the other facts, both the geographic and historic facts have a symbolic value which obviously does not take anything away from their reality as facts, but which confers on them, in addition to this immediate reality, a superior significance.'

Jean Marquès-Rivière, the young orientalist and profound connoisseur of things Tibetan, in his passionate account of Tibetan initiatic doctrines,[1] has not only 'materialised' this initiatic centre, but also 'localised' it in a hidden land, Napamako. This forbidden land, or rather

---

[1]*In the Shadow of Tibetan Monasteries* (published by Attinger).

this occult centre, hidden from the eyes of 'mortals', seems to be found in the Himalaya, for legend has it that 'Brahmaputra, the holy river, surrounds it in order to protect it'.

J. Marquès-Rivière's guru[1] said: 'In your dark West, turn your thoughts towards Lap-chi-kang.[2] That is where the Guardians of the Human Race keep watch. Meditate on them, meditate on the Gods of the Himalaya and they will thus be visible to you; invisible and solitary, filled with compassion for Humanity, they keep watch until the hour of Dawn and Deliverance.[3]

'… It is again in Tibet, "at the holy Lake of Four Rivers", to the west of Everest,* that we can "give a locality" to one of the forbidden centres or, to put it better, invisible centres, for the "Presences" manifest themselves only to divine eyes'. Their action is all the more powerful because no earthly contingencies disturb them. It is to these powerful Beings that the long descriptions to be found in certain mantra rituals are attributed. It must be pointed out that they are not gods, but far superior to gods.[4]

'However the other tradition is just as well defined. There exist Human Beings on whom Almighty Wisdom and Almighty Power are based. According to Asiatic traditions these are the recluses known to nobody, isolated in

[1]Guru: Spiritual Master.

[2]Tibetan name for the Himalaya.

[3]J. Marquès-Rivière, 'The State of Buddha', in *Theosophical Review*, February 1929.

[4]According to Asiatic tradititions, the gods are still part of manifestation. The beings that I am talking about here, being freed, are beyond or above manifestation, and are therefore higher than the gods. (J.M.R.)

*Lake Manasarovar, beneath Mt Kailas, is north-west of Everest, but the area is famous for containing the source of the four rivers Sutlej, Indus, Brahmaputra and Karnali.

the snowy abysses and inaccessible places of the Himalaya. Thus, throughout Asia, there exists an immense Fraternity; no earthly image can give any idea of this and no
description can be applied to it.

'Hindus have told me strange facts on this subject. I will
mention only the following one:

'About every ten years, in India, either in the North
or in the South, a very large gathering of Yogis and Wise
Men of India takes place. From the North come the Sâd-
hus covered in dust and the naked ascetics, and from the
South come the religious beggars, the forest hermits. In
the midst of this multitude a being appears, mounted on
an elephant. This Being blesses his People and strength-
ens them in their search for Eternal Wisdom. The English
Government was worried about this absolutely unforesee-
able gathering of people. They saw it, with terror, as an
element of possible trouble and revolt; but their efforts in
finding the cause of these strange gatherings were in vain.

'The gathering is never announced in advance and yet
the crowd of pilgrims is faithful to the set date. What is
this Being? Where is he from? The mystery still rules supreme in Asia...'.[1]

Is this the Sovereign Pontiff of Asia? Indeed, Saint-Yves
d'Alveydre[2] describes a mysterious figure who appears at
certain ceremonies as follows: 'Mounted on a white elephant, he streams with a dazzling, blinding light from his
crown to his feet, and surrounded by similar scintillations,
but it is difficult to distinguish his features from those of

[1]Note by Mr J. Marquès-Rivière
[2]Saint-Yves d'Alveydre, *The Mission of India*. p. 97. Dorbon-Ainé,
Paris.

other pontiffs, for his face is veiled by a fringe of diamonds reflecting all of the sun's rays'.

What is more, this author situates Agartha, the partly underground temple whose name means 'elusive to violence', 'impervious to anarchy', in Asia, in the Himalaya: 'It is sufficient for my readers to know that, in certain regions of the Himalaya, among the 22 Temples representing the 22 Arcanas of Hermes and the 22 letters of certain holy alphabets, Agartha forms the mystic zero: the Unobtainable…'

In her strange visions,[1] Catherine Emmerich, a Nun in the Augustinian Convent of the Dulmen (in Germany) also seemed to situate the Mountain of Wise Ones, of Prophets, in the Himalaya. She placed her Agartha on an island in the middle of a lake at the top of a mountain: 'It is there, on this mountain, the highest in the world,[2] where nobody is able to go, that treasures and holy mysteries were put in a secure place when corruption grew among men. The lake, the island, and the towers exist only so that these treasures should be conserved and guaranteed beyond reach'.

Mr R. Guénon, again in his masterly *King of the World*, links this mysterious Agartha tradition with Christianity as proof of its perfect orthodoxy regarding the primordial

[1]'The Life of Anne-Catherine Emmerich' by Father Schmoeger. This Nun was born in 1773 and died in 1819, a time when the question of Agartha was not a preoccupation of the Western mind. In addition, no Catholic tradition mentions a Mountain of Prophets or anything connected with one.

[2]'The Life of A.-C Emmerich' edited by Téqui in 1925, says on page 189: 'In the second week of Advent, Anne-Catherine was led by her angel to the highest peak of a mountain in Tibet, which is in fact inaccessible. She saw, guarded by Elie, the treasures of all the divine knowledge communicated to man by angels since the beginning of the world…'

Tradition represented, in the case in point, by the Three Wise Men: the Three Wise Ones of Agartha.

'On this subject, we will clarify a point which seems never to have been satisfactorily explained, that of the 'Three Wise Men' of the Gospel uniting in themselves the two Powers; we will say now that these three mysterious characters are none other than the three Chiefs of Agartha. The Mahanga offers Christ Gold and hails him King, the Mahâtma offers him Incense and hails him Priest, and the Brahâtma offers him Myrrh (the balm of incorruptibility, image of the Amritâ) and hails him Prophet or Spiritual Master *par excellence*.'

Mohammed also seems to allude to the tradition of Agartha when he speaks in the Koran of 'Companions of the Cave' (Sura XVIII, verse 8). Indeed it is a strange coincidence that, on their subject, he uses the numeral symbolism 3-6-9 (verse 21): 'There will be disagreement on how many of them there were. One person will say there were three and their dog was the fourth. Another will say there were five and their dog was the sixth. The mystery will be carefully looked into. Another will say there were seven of them and their dog was the eighth'. If these numbers are added together the sum will be 33, the number from which the Cabalistic combination 3-6-9 is derived.

In another verse (24, Sura XVIII), also concerning the Companions of the Cave, the Cabalistic trinomial is again clearly used: 'These young people remained in their Cavern for 300 years plus 9'.

It is indeed strange to see that this trinomial plays a considerable role in Islamic symbolism: Mohammed died in the year 9 of the Hegira (631 of the Christian era), during which he made his last pilgrimage to Mecca. On the day of sacrifices he personally slew 63 camels and freed 63 slaves. Mohammed died at the age of 63 (the years being based on lunar months).

Were the Three Wise Ones ⚠ ⚠ ⚠ in the Oracle's replies thus the Three Wise Ones of the Himalaya, the Three Wise Ones, Chiefs of Agartha? That was what we asked.

QUESTION: Are they the Three Wise Ones of Agartha?[1]

REPLY: The Three Wise Ones are the Little Lights who live far from all and near to all.

We were profoundly surprised by this reply. In the luminous hierarchy used by the method, this description of 'Little Lights' did not seem to us to indicate the Three Wise guardians of the Dazzling Astral Force. There was in this an absolute lack of balance between their noble initiatic burden and the description used with respect to them. The very phrase 'living far from all and near to all', while it indicated the Wise Ones having attained a high initiatic and spiritual level, excluded the possibility of a definition of the Supreme Wise Ones as understood by the various traditions. Did our correspondents intend to evoke, then, the mysterious figure of the Supreme Wise One, the King of the World, when they used the descriptions 'Almighty', 'the Greatest Light' and 'the Inconceivable'? We asked this question.

QUESTION: Is the Inconceivable the King of the World, or God as human beings understand it?

REPLY: To want to call the Inconceivable the King

---

[1] We must admit that this question was very badly written, causing the very indirect reply of the 'Little Lights'.

of the World is to be delirious. Men do not know nor can understand, for their brain is insufficient. Sometimes it is only the spirit that feels the whole immensity of it.

QUESTION: Does the King of the World exist?

REPLY: Imagination. Illusion, illusion.

This reply demolished, precisely and clearly and with no 'oracular' ambiguity whatsoever, the Hindu and Tibetan legend of the 'reflection of God', Master of the World, and of its destinies. But should we have considered the tradition of an initiatic hierarchy leading to the Three Supreme Wise Ones, Chiefs of Agartha, as equally demolished: a tradition whose existence was affirmed – almost proven – by so many esoteric and exoteric traditions? We could not accept this. M. Vivian du Mas, the eminent esotericist of a Theosophical study group, had already conducted 'psychic' research on this subject which was very interesting, and from which it was found that Father Julian was in fact one of the Little Lights, hierarchically subordinate to the Supreme Wise Ones.

In addition, a question asked a few days after M. du Mas's communication – a question completely unconnected with the subject in which we were interested – confirmed the results of this esotericist's 'experiments'.

QUESTION: Where is the Master who could save my son, mentally and physically?

REPLY: Your son has around him Powers without light, which are driving the pain even deeper into his heart; it is absolutely essential to ward them off. Try imploring help from the Little Light, Julian △̇ .

The symbol △̇ accompanying the definition of the

hierarchical degree of the 'Little Light Julian' could have led to confusion (being exactly the same as that of one of the Supreme Wise Ones), but the fact that Father Julian was found to be in Bagnaia for atonement was ample proof to us that he could not be one of the supreme Chiefs of this mysterious Agartha. Truly, how could it be said that one of the Guardians of the World could have left the 'Cloisters of Light' in Agartha in order to find a place for his atonement in a humble abandoned cabin in this far-off village of Latium? The supreme Wise Ones, highest spiritual expression of the Initiatic Centre of the World, no longer *atone*; pain and penitence are no longer the lot of those who, having reached the summit of the mountain of blinding Light, 'listen to and record the Word of the Eternal'.

However, despite this reply, we still had no precise and clear confirmation (as clear as that which denied the existence of the King of the World) on the subject of Agartha and the Three Wise Ones. The net of replies still gathered around this point of culmination, but we had not yet dared to construct the definitive questions. Finally, we were so tired of examining hypothesis upon hypothesis, tradition upon tradition and of meditating on the communications and symbols all leading to confirmation of the existence of this Initiatic Centre of the World that we decided to interrogate our Correspondents:

QUESTION: Do the Three Supreme Wise Ones and Agartha exist?

REPLY: The Three Wise Ones exist and are the guardians of the mystery of life and death. After forty winters spent in penitence for sinful humanity and in sacrifices for suffering humanity, special mis-

sions may be undergone that allow entrance into the garden of preparation for the final selection, which opens the door of Agartha.

No: we had not been mistaken: the hierarchies of the Wise Ones and of Agartha are not just visionaries' dreams; they exist. This definition of the Three Wise Ones as guardians of the mystery of life and death fully indicates, without any trace of doubt, the three Supreme Sages. The mystery of life and death is the revelation of the supreme initiation; it is the key to the harmony of macrocosm and microcosm, the insane dream of so many wise men and occultists who ended in madness in their vertiginous race towards this abyss of absolute knowledge: omniscience. The 'Garden of Preparation' is the garden in which the various initiatic 'flowers' bloom; the garden of the Lotus Rose, where all traditions of the World are gathered together and in the middle of which stands, majestically, the sacred Mountain, inviolate dwelling place of the Three.

In the 40 winters[1] of penitence and sacrifice we find, in addition to the symbolic number of penitence, the very

[1]The number 40, says Lacuria, 'is the complete and sufficient period required to complete a work". It is in this sense that one should understand the 40-day fasts of young Eli and of Jesus, Adam's 40-year repentance after his corrupt practices, the length of the deluge and that of the subsequent sterility of the earth, the Jews' 40 years in the Desert and the 40 emissaries of Canaan. As 4 is the number of ordeal, in a way 40 represents the preliminaries of preparation. Jesus was presented in the Temple on the 40th day after his birth, he preached for 40 months, rested 40 hours in the sepulchre and 40 days on Earth after his resurrection. Buddha and Mohammed both began their teaching at the age of 40.The Jews had a 40-day celebration, as the Christians have for Lent. This is a cycle, though always difficult, being limited by natural reactions. Nineveh had had 40 days to repent. (*The Symbolism of Numbers*, Dr R. Allendy (1921)).

Christian initiatic theory of the ascetic – suffering and penitence offered in total sacrifice of one's life to God.

This is perhaps further proof of the Christian leanings of the group with which we are in communication, though it is confirmation also, and first and foremost, of the existence of Agartha – which, with its Garden of Preparation and its Supreme Wise Ones, dominates the initiatic traditions of the world.

Do these Masters possess the enormous power attributed to them by Vedic traditionalists, Theosophists, visionaries and Eastern and Western esotericists? This we are not able to say. Whether Masters of the Three Worlds (according to the Tibetan definition) or Guardians of Life and Death (according to our Correspondents' definition), they seem to be, in fact, supreme guardians of Traditions – who have kept, and still keep, in the innermost reaches of their many teachings, the Utterance of the Ineffable: the One Word.

Finally, a communication obtained following research into the Babylonian oracles should show Agartha, with its Supreme Wise Ones, in its true light, by making us sense the tremendous role played by this initiatic Centre in the history of the World.

It was a question concerning the characters used by the Babylonian Wise Men,[1] in which the Method of Astral Force was written, Aramaic characters being adopted by the Chaldeans only from the 7th century BC on, and Cuneiform script not lending itself to the application of the Method's rules. This is what was asked:

QUESTION: In what sort of characters was the Babylonian Method of Astral Force written?

[1]See page 123.

REPLY: Origin △ ⑥ ⑨ . With the characters of the peoples who were using it.

This communication did not reply directly to the question we had formulated, but its importance is such that it exceeds the modest scope of these notes. Indeed, in addition to the formal indication that people other than the Egyptians and the Chaldeans used the Oracle of Astral Force, there was also the very precise indication that Agartha, with its Wise Ones △ ⑥ ⑨ , was the original Centre and, consequently, the inspirer[1] of certain Oracles that dominated the Ancient World. If we now take into account the tremendous hold Oracles such as those of Delphi, Horus and Bel Marduk (to mention just those of the 'Very Green' basin*) have had upon the history of peoples, we must arrive at a truly impressive conclusion. It is that from the very depths of mysterious Asia, the Supreme Wise Ones dictated, through the mouths of different Gods, 'but all bearing the signs of the Light', the course of history of this ancient world which we know through legends and man-made monuments.

This was an impressive communication which, as we have said, is beyond the very modest scope of these notes, but which, despite this, forced us to remember that when the voice of the 'Light without Equal' – of Christ, of the Sun God of Christian Cabalists, arose there, from the land of the Chosen People, 'the oracles were dumb'. Must we not find in this consideration new proof of the perfect

[1]The Oracles of Astral Force being exactly that, a way of communication with the Initiatic Centre of the World.

*The meaning is unclear: maybe, the fertile lands which formed the cradle of civilisation.

orthodoxy of the mission of Christ in respect of Primordial Tradition? The voices of Mysterious Asia ceased in a sign of homage to, and adoration of, Him for whom they had prepared the Coming into the Roman world.[1]

[1]We say clearly 'in the Roman world'; did not the Eagles of Rome indicate by their superb and powerful flight the borders of the first Kingdom of Christ?

'HE WHO WAITS'

The Man sent by the Inconceivable
Symbolism of 'He Who Waits'
His Cabalistic Definition
His Mission – The Sign of Light

'HE WHO WAITS'

About four years ago we noticed for the first time, in a communication of a prophetic character, a fairly precise reference to the 'Instructor' awaited by certain esoteric circles: *'Living in this period of general chaos, you must follow the destiny of the whole of humanity, which struggles in spasms of madness. Another OOOO and another OOOO[1] until the coming of the Man sent by the Inconceivable to give back to the Human Race the purpose of its existence and the true feeling of that for which one comes into the world…'*

This communication was followed, shortly afterwards, by another ending thus: *'Work with determination and tenacity until you are acquainted with He Who Waits…'*

QUESTION: Who is He Who Waits?

REPLY: Today he is unknown and afar, but tomorrow he will be a Great One by the will of the Most High…

There could be no doubt: 'the Man sent by the Inconceivable' and 'He Who Waits' were two definitions of the same entity.

QUESTION: When will we meet He Who Waits?

REPLY: Many, many moons will pass before you meet He Who Waits…

(reply obtained in November 1925)

The communications concerning 'He Who Waits' continued for a year (1926), interspersed with replies to other

[1]Each circle must correspond to one year.

questions: 'Everything will come to you from He Who Waits…' 'You will meet him when the time is right…' 'You will do that when you meet He Who Waits…'

The following is the penultimate communication concerning 'the Man sent by the Inconceivable'.[1] The interrogation was carried out by an esoteric scholar and the commentaries which follow are his own.

QUESTION: Is He Who Waits the last Avatar or the future Manu?

REPLY: It can be neither one nor the other. The Little Light Unam will perhaps sense it for you…

'The last Avatar is the manifestation of the Word at the end of the present Cycle or Manvantara, a manifestation represented under the symbolic figure of the White Horse in the Puranas and in the Apocalypse. It could be supposed that "He Who Waits" designated, in an enigmatic way, this Avatar; or perhaps, following another equally possible hypothesis, he is the future Manu, that is to say the Intelligence which must rule over the next human cycle and give it its law. However, some previous replies concerning "He Who Waits" makes one think that it was, in reality, something much less important, a non-defined manifestation, playing only a secondary role; but it was interesting to have confirmation of it, and it is this confirmation which this present reply brings most clearly and most positively.

'*Unam* is the reversal of Manu, indicating that it is a reflection of Manu. There exist other known examples of this

[1]The last communication about 'He Who Waits' dates from July 1929. It confirms the coming of this Master who will be the Supreme Spiritual Commander of the 'Polaires'. See Appendix, page 159.

process, such as the name ROMA, considered the reversal of AMOR ; this case seems to have been interpreted in the same way in certain esoteric traditions. *Unam* is qualified as "piccola Luce" – "little Light" – which places it, in a way, at the same level as the "Three Wise Ones", but its name indicates a more direct connection with the "Centre of the World".'

SYMBOLISM OF 'HE WHO WAITS' – We have found, in a personal communication, the symbolic definition of 'He Who Waits', a particularly interesting definition, as much for the entity it designates as for the symbolic form used.

This is the sentence that concluded the communication in question:

'Have confidence in He Who Waits " ⟨12⟩ ⟨13⟩ △ ".'

These three triangles were followed by a rectangle containing the following signs:

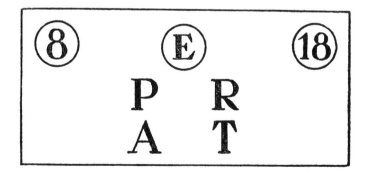

In this symbol two very distinct parts can be discerned:

(1) The spiritual part, indicated by the 3 Triangles;

(2) That of the manifestation on the 'physical plane' indicated by the rectangle and the letters and numbers written inside it.

SYMBOLISM OF THE SPIRITUAL PART – This part is the simpler of the two, for the numbers 12 and 13, written inside the two triangles, signify the 12 doors of Initiation and the Death and Resurrection of Initiation (13). The 'pure' triangle indicates the very high spiritual level of this Initiation, also designating a Master, a Wise One of a very elevated Hierarchy.

SYMBOLISM OF THE 'MANIFESTATION ON THE PHYSICAL PLANE' PART – This part, on the contrary, was very difficult for us to understand, and it was only after very long research that we found the thread of its profound symbolism. The letters A P E R T, read in a circular fashion, gave us the word APERTA, but its Italian or Latin meaning, 'open', did not interest us from an esoteric point of view. The numbers 8 and 18, examined from 'three directions', did not give us sufficient indication to consider them as having a distinctive and 'out of context' meaning. We thus decided to translate the letters and numbers into the phonetically corresponding letters of the Hebrew alphabet. This translation gave us the first key to the strange symbolism of 'He Who Waits' for, read hieroglyphically, they indicated to us the purpose of his coming and his 'earthly attributes':

A = Aleph	Hieroglyphic interpretation:	Power
P = Pe	ditto	Sound

E = He	ditto	Religion
R = Resh	ditto	Command
T = Teth	ditto	Wisdom
8th letter = Heth	ditto	Justice
18th letter = Sadhe	ditto	Purpose

The outcome, given that the two numbers 8 and 18 (the letters Heth and Sadhe) and the letter E (He) were written inside circles – constituting, in this way, the dominant part of this symbolism – is that we read:

The Purpose of the Coming of 'He Who Waits' is RELIGION* and JUSTICE (the Supreme Good) and that to attain this goal he possesses: SOUND, WISDOM, COMMAND and POWER. Thus it seems to us that the definition of 'The One sent by the Inconceivable' could not be more precise or more complete.[1]

Despite this, we wanted to penetrate the symbolic sense of the word APERTA, certain that it had not been put there only for its letters to be translated into Hebrew. It must have a meaning of its own which we looked for in vain in modern Latin dictionaries.

It was only one year after having received this interesting symbolic communication that we found the exact signification of this word, in an old dictionary, 'Totius Latinitatis Lexicon' by Forcellini. 'APERTA', explained this dignified 18th century ecclesiastic, 'inquit Festus, Apollo

[1]This symbolism indicates the great responsibility with which the Supreme Chief of the 'Polaires' is invested.

*The word 'Religion' is a straight rendering of the same word in French. It seems here to carry a sense, present in the Latin, of bonding, just as a community or brotherhood is bound together. 'Sound' has been chosen for 'Pe' to represent the French 'Parole'. 'Pe' carries the sense of anything that comes out of the mouth: speech, promise, Word.

vocabatur, quia patente cortina responsa ab eo darentur'. Thus Apollo was called 'Aperta' so that he answered to 'cortina aperta',[1] clearly and without oracular ambiguity.[2] We had here the key to the second enigma, for we found in this God – the Sun God and God of Light – the luminous Tradition of the Method of Astral Force, and the indication that 'He Who Waits' indeed came among men under the sign of Helios. In addition, Apollo being the God of Divination, the Father, Brother or Husband of the Sybils, the protective and inspiring god of Sibylline Oracles, and with his evocation in the symbolism of 'He Who Waits', came, in a sense, to reinforce the oracular character of the Method. This double interpretation of the Apollonian symbolism led us to very important research on the Sibylline Oracles and to connect their Solar Tradition to that, equally solar, of the Horus Oracles in Egypt and of the Bel Marduk Oracles in Babylon.

---

[1]'Patente cortina': literally 'in an open pot'. Indeed the tripod was called pot because of its resemblance to this domestic utensil. ('Totius Latinitatis Lexicon', E. FORCELLINI, Paravii, 1771)

[2]Apollo always spoke in his name and in the first person. He liked to disconcert his clients a little, to hide his thoughts under metaphors, enigmas and double entendres. He also liked to moralise and some of his replies are impressions of the highest philosophy. (E. SAGLIO, 'Dictionary of Greek and Roman Antiquity').

ORACLES OF ANTIQUITY

Delphi and the Sibylline Oracles of Astral Force
The Babylonian Oracle of Astral Force
Bel Marduk
Symbolism of Bel Marduk
The Oracle of Horus

ORACLES OF ANTIQUITY

I
DELPHI AND THE SIBYLLINE ORACLES
OF ASTRAL FORCE

Struck by the symbolism '3-6-9' found in the offer of the Sibylline books by the Cumaean Sybil to Tarquinius Superbus[1] and by certain similarities between the written procedure of the Method of Astral Force and the written method of certain Apollonian Oracles (very closely linked to Sibylline Oracles), we formulated the following question:

QUESTION: Please tell us if the Sibylline Oracles were obtained by the Method of Astral Force.

REPLY: Some of these Oracles were obtained by inspiration caused by a special atmosphere and the others were Oracles of Astral Force.

Indeed, near the Tripods (caves with inspiring vapours[2],

---

[1]The first time, the Sybil offered Tarquinius 9 books, which he refused; the second time, 6, which he also refused; and the third time, 3, which he finished by buying. We know that these three books contained only the practical part of the cult, that is indications of the means used to ward off divine anger in extraordinarily perilous circumstances. The first 6 must also have been important, for they were consulted by the Priests at Delphi to create certain Oracles (very probably written ones). Did they contain a divinatory arithmetical Method? This is very possible, taking into account certain similarities in procedure between the Oracles of Astral Force and those of Apollo.

[2]It is in the igneous volcanic nature of the soil that the prophetic spirit operates, by a sort of communication with the internal fire, the arid, reddish land, and the sulphurous emanations.

fountains,[1] rustling of leaves, Chambers of Dreams, Prophetesses and Sibyls) there were the 'Libri Fatales', mysterious books about the Romans' destiny along with the Greeks' Sibylline Books; there were also blades of lead or pewter, tablets framed with laurel leaves on which were engraved or written mortals' questions and the gods' replies, proof that the question and answer were formulated in writing.[2] If we add to this very important observation the fact that the questions were generally submitted in the evening to the god's 'secretary', and that the interested parties could go to collect them only the next day, we find further proof of the slow process common to both oracles.

An extremely interesting indication comes from this communication concerning the Sibylline Oracles. If the Wise Ones of Agartha, of this initiatic omphalos† of the World, were the instigators of the written Oracles of Apollo (Delphi),[3] it is easy to see the immense power exerted by

[1]The Kassotis Fountain in Delphi.*

[2]Normally, the questions were asked in writing on Tablets. The reply was also given in writing (Herodotus). The 'clients' asked their questions verbally, or in writing on a tablet framed with laurel. The one consulting brought the reply on a sealed tablet if he was but an intermediary (Plutarch). Here are two questions asked by the Athenians (engraved on two pewter tablets) and intended for the Delphi Oracle. The manner in which they are composed is reminiscent of those asked of the Oracle of Astral Force which is in the possession of our friend: (a) Would it be better to rent out the pieces of land to make money for the construction of a Temple to Eleusis? (b) Would it be better to leave them overgrown in honour of the Goddesses? (Foucart: Bull. Corr. Hell., XIV, 1890).

[3]Delphi: this oracle served as a model for other oracles and exerted a very powerful influence over the development of the Hellenic civilisation, over its political, religious, colonial, financial and artistic organisation... (Saglio, Dictionary of Greek and Roman Antiquities).

*The Kassotis Fountain sinks into ground and reappears as the better-known Castalian spring.   †I.e., the central point.

them over the Greek, and even Barbarian, world: 'Delphi, the most famous of all Oracles', said Herodotus, 'became the religious metropolis of Greece and the political capital of the peoples who sent representatives to the Amphictyonic Assembly at Delphi. The Barbarians themselves sent ambassadors and offerings to the Delphi temple'.

II
THE BABYLONIAN ORACLE OF ASTRAL FORCE
THE ORACLE OF HORUS

We have seen that the answer to our question 'Is it a form of Cabala?' (see page 67) ended with the indication 'If Ramples was atrociously punished by the Chaldeans, it was because he rebelled against the Demfti Oracle of Astral Force'.[1] We found in this sentence – which seemed to have no connection with the question asked – the procedure dear to our correspondents to put us on track for an interesting communication.[2] In fact it was by basing our judgment on indications of this kind, which seem thrown out as if by accident, that we managed to find the thread of many mysterious tangles. Truly, we must not forget

---

[1] Oracle: in the literal sense the word, oracle (oraculum) designates the answer of a God or a deified hero consulted in a place determined by way of some kind of divination; by extension, and very often, it designates either the authorised interpreters of God, or the Sacerdotal Corporations, etc. (Saglio, *Dictionary of Greek and Roman Antiquities*). The name Demfti is thus the name of the 'authorised' interpreter of the Oracle of Astral Force.

[2] See the communication received on the subject of the writing of the Babylonian Method of Astral Force.

that our correspondents seemed to want us to get used to 'searching for the light with our own eyes and not using theirs to see it', every light having to be acquired by the most persistent work and effort.

We will transcribe here some communications referring to this fascinating Chaldeo-Egyptian question raised by the indication below, communications which permitted us to find, almost certainly, the Babylonian Oracle of Astral Force.

QUESTION: Why do Demfti and Ramples have Egyptian names?[1]

*REPLY: Because they were.**

QUESTION: Is the Oracle of Astral Force found in Egypt or Chaldea?

REPLY: The Oracle of Astral Force exists as much in Egypt as in Babylon.

Following this indication, our research was concentrated around the Babylonian Oracle of Bel Marduk, for we found in this god, Lord of the Babylonian Pantheon,[2] the Solar Tradition of the Method and, in his Oracle, the writing method constituted by the tablets of Destinies he wore around his neck and which he used to read the destinies of Gods and of Men; he dictated these destinies to God Nabou, his son, who wrote on the tablets, which were then communicated to the interested

---

[1]These Egyptian names connected with Chaldean initiatic history should not be surprising. The Chaldean Wise Men did not exclude outsiders as a matter of course from their initiation and their teachings. What is more, we have an example in the fact that Daniel was appointed Archimage under Nebuchadnezzar.

[2]Bel Marduk was the Sun God of Babylonian cosmology.

*I.e., they *were* Egyptian.

party.[1] In addition, the symbolism of a Bel Marduk bas-relief[2] seemed to us to be made up in the same way, being identical to that of the Method and by extension to that of Agartha and the Three Wise Ones – another link between the Oracle of Astral Force and that of the Supreme Babylonian God. The symbolism of the bas-relief in question consists of three parts: the first, and most important, is written on the apron of the God; the second on his right arm and the third on his chest. The first consists of three ideograms, written in three circular ornamentations which can be described as follows:

– First ideogram, representing a circular grid : ideogram of the Sun,[3] thus corresponding to the Spirit and the number 3.

– Second ideogram, representing a Wheel or Star with 5 spokes or points: ideogram (as much one as the other) of the Astral and corresponding to the number 6.

– Third ideogram, representing three bulls, two of which are face to face and one resting: ideogram of Matter, of the physical plane, the bull, according to Chaldean Tradition, representing the watery principle from which the first

[1]The 'Tablets of Destinies' did not constitute a symbol but a real hierarchical accessory of God, indispensable to assure the investiture to the grade of Supreme Babylonian God. Hammourabi the Reformer (3rd Century B.C.) dispossessed Enlil, the Supreme Chaldean God, of this grade solemnly to accord it to Bel Marduk so that Bel Marduk should become Lord of the Gods in place of Enlil.

[2]This bas-relief is found in the Berlin Pre-Asiatic Museum.

[3]The Grid is either the imitation of the screen, the creative sieve of the small suns, or the image of the collection of squared, linked discs, and consequently an increase in solar power and solar heat. This chequered disc is the Summer Sun, the Sun of Fire (Emile SOLDI, The Holy Tongue, Paris 1897).

living beings were born by spontaneous generation. In the two bulls face to face and the one at rest is also found the representation of three inferior forces which concur with the formation of matter. Ideogram corresponding to the number 9.

SYMBOLISM ON THE RIGHT ARM OF THE GOD – The god wears on his right arm 9 stars, encrusted in lapis lazuli, as are the three ideograms described above. It is easy, in these 9 stars, to discover the Cabalistic progression 3-6-9, but what is particularly important is that, in the Method, the operations of the onomantic* phase are also indicated by 9 stars.

SYMBOLISM FOUND ON THE GOD'S CHEST – On the god's chest can be seen a certain number of stars, impossible to count exactly as they have been partly worn away with time.[1] It is very possible that they are the 33 Constellations which were originally under Enlil's command and of which Bel Marduk, as successor of the Supreme God, had taken possession. In this case, we would find here the symbol of the Astral as dissected by us for the numerical ideogram of the Method (see page 146).

Therefore, is not the identity of signification of two symbolic languages – whatever the graphic form in which they are expressed – certain proof of the link between them and, in this case, proof of their common origin? Consequently, we consider that the Bel Marduk Oracle, the importance of which in the ancient world is pointed out

---

[1] The description of this bas-relief was obligingly communicated to us by the Berlin Pre-Asiatic Museum.

*I.e., numerical.

by Plutarch in his 'Life of Alexander' and by Arrian in his 'Anabasis', was indeed the Babylonian Oracle of Astral Force. Here is our question on this subject, and the corresponding reply:

QUESTION: *Pray tell us if the Oracle of Bel Marduk really was the Babylonian Oracle of Astral Force.*

REPLY: *Oracle of Astral Force Tres.*

Should we have considered the word 'Tres' as a signature to the reply or did it have another meaning? This is what we asked:

QUESTION: *Pray tell us the meaning of the word Tres.*

REPLY: *The true meaning of this word cannot be grasped by a Western brain.*

However, our mysterious correspondents were much more precise on the subject of the Egyptian Oracle of Astral Force:

QUESTION: *What is the Egyptian Oracle of Astral Force called?*

REPLY: *Oracle of Gold.*

It was Hor, Horus, Son of Isis and Osiris, the Egyptian Sun God, God of divination, who with 9 (female) musicians travelled all over Egypt to bring civilisation to it.

In this God we found the Solar Tradition of the Method and the Cabalistic trinomial represented by the 'nine musicians', but we had insufficient time to go deeper into the question of the written method. However, this God reminded us of Apollo of the Greeks and his Sibylline Oracles too much to have any doubts on the validity of this communication. Also, on the subject of this God, we find it interesting to indicate the strange coincidences existing between the Bel Marduk Oracle and that of Delphi:

1)   The same numeral symbolism: 3-6-9, symbol of the Oracle of Astral Force and which is found in the symbolic offer of the Cumaean Sybil to Tarquinius Superbus: 9 books, 6 books, and 3 books.

2)   The same Solar Tradition: Bel Marduk was the Sun in the Babylonian cosmogony just as Apollo was the Sun (Phoebus) in the Greek.

3)   The same special atmosphere for the oral Oracles: (a) the Chamber of Dreams in the Ziggurat at Esagil, dedicated to Bel Marduk and occupied by the earthly wife of this God (she gave the oral Oracles while explaining her dreams); (b) Apollo's Temple where the Pythian prophetess went into a trance, under the influence of emanations from the Tripod, to give the oral Oracles of the God.

4)   The same written method: Tablets of Destinies in the case of Bel Marduk and Sibylline books in the case of Apollo.

FURTHER COMMUNICATIONS

Buddha – Confucius – Krishnamurti
War – Kala-Nag, the Black Serpent
Shambala – The dream – Moksha
The Five Routes – Ananda
The interferences – Ariosto
The Wise Knights – The Sign of Signs

FURTHER COMMUNICATIONS

We transcribe below some replies obtained in Paris in January 1929, as well as those, old and recent, which may better enlighten the reader on the luminous, geometric and numerical symbolism used by our Correspondents.

QUESTION: Who is Buddha? Is his path right?

REPLY: Buddha is a Great Light. All paths which lead to Light are good.

We repeat that Christ is defined by our Correspondents as 'Light without equal', whereas Confucius is said to be 'The Divine',[1] and Socrates is also called 'Great Light' and Mohammed 'The Great Warrior of Medina' or 'The Great Prophet of the Eternal Black Stone'. Should we consider all of these definitions as an indication of how our Correspondents regard them? We think so.

QUESTION: Pray tell us, who is Krishnamurti?

REPLY: He is not a Wise One. He will hasten the severe punishment which must purify Humanity.

This communication, signed by an entity of the highest spirituality (the 3 in the Yod of celestial writing), denied, to present Humanity, the two superior planes of the Microcosm, with the following symbols. The symbols of these two planes[2] were, in fact, replaced by two squares

---

[1] This is the communication in which the name of Confucius is mentioned: '*Confucius the Divine said: Lower your head humbly and your humility will become a force strong enough to hit hard he who made you lower it*'. Here, one should take the adjective 'Divine' in the Latin sense of the word.

[2] The symbolic synthesis of the Microcosm (and of the Macrocosm) consists of the Triangle (the Spirit), the Circle (the Astral) and the square (Matter).

with the sign of Imperfection (the number 2). Here is the symbolism in question:

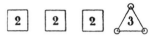

What is the severe punishment prepared by the Eternal for the people of the Earth? Is it War? Should we compare this communication to the one concerning War received in 1926?

QUESTION: Is it War?

REPLY: The Fatal Comet which will plunge Humanity into limitless pain to permit it to find the Route to follow is still far away.

As we have already said – just as in the Sibylline Oracles – our Correspondents attributed War to the influence of a Comet.

On the subject of the same symbolism, we will cite the reply obtained in May 1918 concerning the end of that War.

QUESTION: When will it end? (the War)

REPLY: The Fatal Comet is starting to distance itself from the Earth's orbit. The first snow will warm the wheat of Peace.[1]

QUESTION: Should I continue to follow the path I sense?

REPLY: The path you sense cannot be the right one, for Kala-Nag ☐2☐ *will <u>divert</u> you.*

S

⟠

The importance of this communication is considerable, as much in the evocation of Kala-Nag (the Black Serpent,

---

[1]Note that the sowing period falls in November.*

*The Armistice was signed on 11 November 1918.

the Black King) as a Human Entity as in its really interesting symbolic whole.

On the subject of Kala-Nag, the following interesting note was given to us by Mr J. Marquès-Rivière: 'Kala-Nag is a Sanskrit word composed of Kala and Nag. Each of these having multiple meanings, it would be best to study them before giving a complete interpretation. Kala, or rather Kal, signifies the Supreme Spirit seen as the destructor of the Universe; this would be the Christian Satan, but even more grandiose, for, following the example of the Black God of the Cabalists, it is one of the aspects of the Demiurge. It has a sense of death, of fatal destiny; Kali, a feminine form, has a sense of darkness, of night. This is Parvati, wife of Shiva, and for those who know the nature of Shiva, his passive side can only be fearsome and frightening; it is one of the forms of White Durga,* 'she who is approached with difficulty'. Finally, it is one of the sisters of Yama, the God of Hell and Death. *Nag* also has multiple meanings: it is the Serpent, the Sun, the number 7, the Mountain; it is the Master, the Wise One, he who possesses frightening esoteric knowledge. On its own it has no evil meaning but, associated with Kala, the sign of Darkness, the meaning becomes horrifying: it is the Black King, Satan, the principle of differentiation *par excellence*. It seems, according to the strange symbol of communication (the 2 inside the square), that it is a human being. Therefore the complete meaning of the Sanskrit word seems to apply to an exceptionally evil human being such as the Antichrist of the Apocalypse. This would be the human reflection of Darkness, a Black Prince, opposed to

---

*'White Durga' is a name given to Parvati herself.

the reflection of light residing in other humans.'

We have said that the symbolism of this communication, a symbolism consisting of two geometric figures and the letter S written under the words 'will divert' is particularly interesting. Indeed:

1)   The 2 written inside the square indicates that Kala-Nag is an imperfect entity of the physical plane but whose imperfection should be understood in its pejorative sense, basely material. Even more important than Kala-Nag until now, the Black Serpent was held by esotericists as a 'Force', or as a symbol of this Force, whereas in this communication it appears, we repeat, as an Entity of the physical plane: probable chief of a Sect of Black Wise Men, the inversed hypostasis of one of the Supreme Wise Ones;

2)   The diamond shape with the cross represents the sign of the astral vortex (the cross representing precisely the rotation of this geometric projection). But, in this case, it is the vortex of inferior forces, as is indicated by the place in which it is found: under the name of Kala-Nag. We will see below how the physical vortex is symbolised;

3)   The letter 'S' corresponds to the Hebrew letter 'salech', whose Cabalistic and hieroglyphic meaning is that of destiny, fatality. It thus indicates that the questioner will be fatally diverted from his path. In addition, the letter 'salech' corresponds to the 15th card of the Tarot: the Devil. So we can say that this letter resumes the reply in part, for it indicates fatality and designates Kala-Nag: the Devil.

Here is another communication referring to the symbol of the vortex (in the physical plane).

QUESTION: I wish to have news of 'X', who dis-

appeared 15 years ago.

REPLY: He was engulfed by a fatal vortex ⌂.

Here the diamond shape with the cross is surrounded by four 4s (the cube) to indicate clearly that it is a vortex in the physical plane, and in this case the vortex certainly was in the physical plane because the person ('X') had disappeared at sea following an accident. This reply confirmed a mysterious death.

QUESTION: Which Path leads to Shambala?

REPLY: In Moulmein[1] lives old Ligh △₃ who teaches the path to the one who brings the Word of Wisdom.

The Word of Wisdom should be considered here in the physical sense of the word, for the 3 is written under the base of the triangle (the base indicating the physical plane). Shambala, according to the Central Asian tradition, is a holy town which, in very ancient times, would have disappeared and become subterranean; some suppose that it was a city buried beneath the Gobi desert, while others would situate it in Siberia. In reality, it is said that Shambala was in a very northern region, and the parallel one can draw with other traditions in this respect allows its identification in the hyperborean Thule, starting point of the primitive tradition in the present Manvantara. This name can also be taken as one of the multiple designations of the 'Centre of the World', and any attempt at giving it a location would be completely in vain; the expression 'a path leading to Shambala' should be understood in a purely symbolic sense. It is strange that, according to the reply given, the one who teaches the path lives in

[1]Moulmein in Burma.*

*Now known as Mawlamyne.

Burma; one would have rather expected to find him in Tibet, where indications concerning Shambala seem much more widespread.

Finally, here is the translation of some questions of a personal nature which nonetheless afford a real philosophical and initiatic interest.

QUESTION: Have I done well? Have I done badly?

REPLY: Imperfect but beloved son, your first thought was such that it completely invalidated your work of redemption. But I had confidence in you. I knew that the feeling of vengeance was on your lips, but not in your soul – and that which you have done and will do is good for you and for your elevation to the Great Throne of the Inconceivable.

QUESTION: Father Julian, may we see you in Bagnaia?[1]

REPLY: Beloved son, I can do no more for you for some time. I have prayed to the Great Light to keep you out of the dangers that threaten, above all, 'X'. Do not call upon me again until the moment when you see me in a dream.

Father Julian appeared in a dream to our friend about 40 days later. He reassured him on a subject that greatly preoccupied him and gave him a communication important to the author. It was during this dream – the only one in which the operator saw Father Julian – that the latter showed our friend his knee, wound round with a yellow handkerchief, saying to him: 'I remember…'

QUESTION: Which combination must I choose?

---

[1]Bagnaia: the small region where our friend had met Father Julian. Those 'who know' will understand this question.

REPLY: You must not, nor cannot, choose, for nothing that happens to you will be by your own choice.[1] A Force which was △2 △3, is acting on you and for you. It is this Force that will inspire you in the early hours of the morning. What you will feel, at that moment, that you should do will be the right choice.

The 'Force which Was' is a Being which was materially alive. The numbers 2 and 3 each written in a Triangle, indicate that it is a Spiritual Force having evolved (passage from the 2 of imperfection to the 3 of perfection).

QUESTION: May I have direct communication with you?

REPLY: By refining the spirit, by abandoning all material things. Then ask and you will have the reply through inspiration.

This communication confirmed the existence of our Correspondents and the high spirituality of the Centre to which they belong, a high spirituality that we will find confirmed in the reply concerning moksha (liberation).

QUESTION: Which Path do you advise to reach moksha?

REPLY: Overcome all human passions. Atone and suffer for 'sorrowing' Humanity.

Indeed, how to reach moksha, how to follow the glorious Path which leads to the ONE, the royal Path which the saints, the victorious and the Wise Ones have followed for all time, without freeing oneself from human passions which obscure 'the Spark'* and stop one's elevation to the indefinable plane?

[1]In this case, of course.   *See p. 75 and note.

To take on the karma of men, to bear their physical suf-
ferings – to merge with their soul and their body – this is
the path to reach this goal of Light which Sanskrit texts
call moksha[1] and which Saint Francis of Assisi called 're-
pose in God'.

*QUESTION: Is there not but one path to reach
moksha or, if there are several, which is the one you
consider the best?*

*REPLY: There are five main paths, but they are
difficult to follow, being filled with obstacles.*

These 'main paths' seem to constitute five different ways
of reaching liberation, the indefinable plan.

If we take the religious 'way' as an example, it is obvious that to reach moksha after death is not just to do with
following religious form at its everyday level. To explain
ourselves 'in Christian terms', we will say that, in this
case, the way of Christ would be that of the ascetic Rule
of Saint Francis of Assisi: the Rule which leads the one
who follows it faithfully to the indefinable plane without
having to pass – after death – through purgatory, that is

---

[1]Moksha is a Sanskrit term signifying liberation. In Brahmanic and
also Buddhist terminology this word has a sense that no European language can fully express.

According to traditional Indian understanding, the Universal divides
into two aspects: the Manifested – the sensible world and the states of
subtle matter – and the Non-Manifested, the World without form: Arûpa.
The first has as characteristics the name and form: nâma-rûpa. The goal
of the Yogi, he who wishes to reach the Non-Manifested, is thus to liberate
himself from the Manifested, from the illusory 'separativity'. In fact, a mi-
rage disguises the manifestation: this is Maya. Yoga is the method used for
this liberation and Moksha is the goal. In Moksha, the Manifested is found
in the Unique: all 'separateness', every affirmation of any 'me' has disappeared. Here are found the Superior States of the Being which no mental
state can conceive, being itself a manifestation. (J. Marquès-Rivière)

to say by the process of expiation indicated in other religious philosophies by reincarnation, survival on different
planes, and so on.

'Paths filled with obstacles'… The mortification of the
flesh, this prison of the Spirit, its lacerations, its suffer-
ings, its tortures, and the sacrifice of its whole being for
others and for God – only these carry the ascetic to the
Supreme God. But they also lead the weak to madness and
the strong to the dizziness of pride. This one collapses in
the painful hell of the physical plane, while the other one
grasps 'the Shadow' in his feverish fingers, believing to
have perceived the Imperceptible… They are paths filled
with obstacles because the Serpent is always there, ready
to precipitate those who thirst for the Spirit towards the
Tree of the Knowledge of Good and Evil.

*QUESTION: In my spiritual anguish, tell me which
Guru will save me; why is there such a wall in front
of me? Where may I find peace?*

*REPLY: First you must acquire merit in helping
those who suffer. You will find Peace in the new Light
which will come to you from Anand, but not before
the 5 circles distance themselves from you, thus deliv-
ering you from the eternal uncertainty and the confusion which deprives you of the Light.*

Anand is the exact transcription in Western phonetics
of the Sanskrit term ânanda, which means beatitude; it

also indicates the 48 years of the Circle of Jupiter. Finally, it is the name of a cousin of Sakyamuni Buddha, the dear disciple of whom he later became.

It must be mentioned that, according to orthodox Brâhmanic Tradition, the inconceivable (Brahma neuter) appears in the Manifested world under a threefold aspect:

1)   Sat (Existence)
2)   Chit (total Awareness)
3)   Ananda (Beatitude)

Thus Ananda is the third aspect. A hasty interpretation could liken it to the Holy Ghost of the Catholic Trinity. It cannot be such, for the planes are totally different and the senses dissimilar. How should the passage of this reply be interpreted…?

Is it a term meaning 'the Blessed One', 'the Beatified One'? Is it a sort of reminder of the dear disciple of Buddha? Note that the beginning of the reply, regarding the acquisition of merits through universal compassion, is pure Buddhism.[1] The name Ananda immediately evokes to all Buddhists the same idea of love, self-sacrifice and the confidential disciple as does St John to a Christian ear. On this subject, it is strange to observe that the replies given to the one consulting the Oracle here have always included Sanskrit words, as if this consultant possessed an Eastern mentality, and is in a way more able to understand the Sanskrit term, in its complex and rich sense, than the precise but limited word in any Western language.

We note here that it is a new Light coming from Ananda. We can liken Ananda to 'He Who Waits', of whom the description of 'Blessed One', of 'Beatified One', is very accurate.

---

[1]Christian and Muslim also (speaking only of 'Western' religions).

QUESTION: Can one reach perfection quicker having a wife one loves with pure love, and does this duality have a chance of becoming one after death?

REPLY: In the true Life of Light there must be no duality. There is only infinite love in all and for all. The most perfect, by Divine Will, can have missions.

The following interrogation was formulated by M. Sudre, scientific writer for *The Journal*, during experimental communications carried out by the operator at the offices of *The Intransigent*.

QUESTION: What is the name of the scientist whose hand I shook today?

REPLY: To 'Knowledge without Love 2'. Why do you ask what you already know? : $2\text{-}2 = \frac{3}{O}$

The translation into French loses a little of the force of the original Italian. Thus it is said to the faithless[1] scientist that the imperfection of this frame of mind (imperfection indicated by the (2) would disappear (2-2) if the Spirit (the 3) dominated the Intellectual Forces (the circle). In this way our Correspondents pay homage to the high intellectuality of the questioner, while refusing to reply to a question which they consider useless.[2]

---

[1]To knowledge without love, that is to say to the scientist without faith.

[2]As we have seen (p. 87), only questions about things of the greatest importance should be asked. However, we did not refuse M. Sudre's request, as we ourselves were tempted by this experiment.

Actually, this reply was far more conclusive for the esotericists present than if it had afforded the 'precision' re-
quested by the questioner.

On the other hand, another question of the same kind
as the one we have just examined permitted us to receive
a really interesting indication on the subject of a possible
interference between ourselves and our Correspondents.

*QUESTION: What exactly is the person I revere
the most, apart from my mother, suffering from?*

*REPLY: If you know, it is useless to ask. If you do
not know, ask with faith so as not to receive erroneous replies. Anselm.*

Through this communication we see that if the questioner does not formulate his question *with faith*, he risks
being misled.[1] By whom? We do know that our Correspondents, when presented with an insufficient telepathic request,[2] suggest that we repeat the question. So why
should we receive erroneous replies? By whom would they
be dictated? There is certainly an indication here of an
interference, always possible between them and us, an
interference by a Group or a Sect living in the shadow
of Kala-Nag and possessing 'magic' means as powerful as
those of the *White* Initiates; and as these Sects are fairly
numerous in Asia, it would not be out of the ordinary for

---

[1]In this case, the interested party, a good friend of ours, admitted having asked this question without concentrating and very rapidly, and he
insisted writing it in this way as an experiment. As we have just seen,
it permitted us to receive a particularly interesting indication. 'Anselm'
must be another Little Light; we think this on the basis of other communications. We will point out that this 'Wise One', like Father Julian, has
a truly Latin name.

[2]Example: '*Ask again with a more tranquil soul.*'

the Black Wise Ones to reply to 'calls' made *without faith*, that is to say to questions asked *without sufficient concentration and without the evocation of the 'method' by which the reply is obtained*[1] (the Oracle of Astral Force).

From among the communications of a purely divinatory nature, we transcribe here two that the Angel of Death covers with his wing.

QUESTION: Where is he? Dead or alive? Shall I see him again?

REPLY: Fatally – I am sorry for it.

Question and reply both in English:* – the 'Fatally' refers, of course, to Death.

QUESTION: Give me news of my Sister.

REPLY: She has passed the Gates of Light.

Here is an example of two questions both written in the same terms by the questioners.

QUESTION: What will be my professional fortune?

REPLY: You must always struggle. In time you will improve your lot if you know how to use to advantage a combination that will be given to you by a woman.

QUESTION: What will be my professional fortune?

REPLY: You will find the answer in the eleventh, twelfth, thirteenth and fourteenth verses of Ariosto.

Through this poetic indication, the questioner is put on his guard, in a very unusual way, against a woman who 'files away his intelligence with every passing hour'…

[1]'Concentration' and 'evocation' always provoke a state of psychic hypersensitivity predisposing active or passive telepathic communications.

*I.e., the question was put in English and the response came in English too.

Che per amor venne in furore e matto
D'uom che si saggio era stimato prima;
Se da colei che tal quasi m'ha fatto
Che l'poco ingegno ad or ad or mi lima…
                    (Ariosto, Orlando furioso, canto 1,
                            from 11th to 14th verse)

These verses may be translated as follows:

'The man who was previously considered so wise became raving mad – and she who had made him so filed
away his intelligence with every passing hour…'*

The manner in which this communication was made is,
at the very least, strange. We will even say that, at first
glance, it surprised us. From the far-off initiatic Centre,
situated in a mysterious corner of Asia, the evocation of
Ariosto seems almost a complete anachronism.[1] But, if we
reflect a little, we will see that this curious way of reply-
ing is fully in line with certain other communications. Are
Anselm and Julian not Latin names? Or, better still, is
their spelling not purely Italian? (Giuliano and Anselmo).
So why be surprised if the Little Lights, Chiefs of an initi-

---

[1]The 'Oracle' of Casanova indicated to the Venetian the day of his
flight from Piombi using the same method: a verse of Ariosto, 'Fra il fin
d'Ottobre e il Capo di Novembre' (between the end of October and the
first of November). It is known that Casanova left his prison in the night
of 30th October/1st November.†

*Orlando furioso was begun in 1506, its 'source' being the twelfth-century
Chanson de Roland ('Orlando'). The lines quoted are from the second stanza of
Canto 1. In T. H. Croker's eighteenth-century translation, the lines read: 'Whom
love to rage and madness did betray, /A man so sage esteem'd in former time;/
If she, who my small wit still files away,/And has reduced me almost like him.'
Note the 'file' image: it is tempting to render this 'wears away', but the Italian is
specific. The Italian title is generally devoid of a capital 'f', as here.

†Piombi translates as 'the Leads' and was the prison from which Casanova
escaped. The date of '30th October' should read '31st October'.

atic group perhaps of a Latin tradition, evoke the memory
of a far-off homeland by honouring he who was not only a
great poet but also an initiate and a Rosicrucian?

Furthermore, it was in April 1929, in a communication
about the Rosicrucians, that we found confirmation of the
existence of a group from the Western and Rosicrucian
Tradition, in the Garden of Preparation of Agartha: the
Great Garden. We will examine later the different reasons
permitting us to affirm that we are, precisely, in direct
communication – through the Oracle of Astral Force –
with this Group. Here, we will merely point out that the
reply in question gave us the initiatic degree of the Rosicrucians and also confirmed to us something of the highest importance, their retreat to Asia. Indeed:

*'Wise Knights initiated into the Great Wheel. – They
were absorbed by the Little Lights of the East. They
have left Traditions in the Great Garden.'*

Mr R. Guénon clearly wanted to give us some information about this communication: 'The title of "Knight" is
well suited to the Rosicrucians, for they migrated to the
Temples to maintain, after their destruction, the attachment of the West to the "Centre of the World". The "Great
Wheel" (translation of the Sanskrit word Mahâchakra)
symbolises the world or nature; the "Initiation" to the
'Great Wheel' corresponds to what was called in antiquity the "little mysteries" (an expression which should

perhaps be likened to the designation "Little Lights"?),
which relates to the possibilities of the human state. This
Initiation really is the one that suits the Knights, that is to
say the Kshatriyas; and, regarding the Rosicrucians, this
information seems perfectly accurate because it ties in
absolutely with that which we have already been able to
obtain from elsewhere.

'The "Great Garden" is the Pardes,* from which come
all Traditions and where they are all maintained; it can, in
a certain general sense, be identified with Agartha. However, Agartha can also be considered as corresponding,
more precisely, to the Centre of this Garden (the Mountain
from which flow the four Rivers), by which the communication of the Human World with the Superior Worlds is
directly established.'

To these indications from one of the masters of esotericism we would add that the 'Great Wheel' corresponds,
with the same meaning of Knowledge or of magic Science,
to the Cabalistic 'Rota' and to the tenth card of the Tarot:
'the Wheel of Fortune'.

We will end this long series of examples with a communication referring to the symbol which we adopted, about
five years ago, for everything connected with the Method:

*The word 'Pardes', from which we derive 'Paradise', comes actually from
the Persian, but here signifies the Jewish Paradise garden. If the earlier identification of 'the Lake of Four Rivers' (p. 100) with Lake Manasarovar is correct, then
the mountain would be Mt Kailas or Kailash, because of the same four rivers.

QUESTION: May I use the symbol?
REPLY: Yes, for you have had a true intuition about it.

It was, indeed, intuition; but today we would have adopted it, this Sign of Signs, with the certitude of its precise meaning.

The Triangle, symbol of all spiritual expressions; geometric projection, plane of the Pyramid of Fire which 'subtle' eyes see shining over Agartha; a symbol which is Vedic, Tantric, Lamaist, Judaic, Chaldean, Islamic and Christian; a symbol defining the spiritual plane, at whatever 'altitudes' it may be; a symbol designating the Unknowable, the Immensity of the Inconceivable and the Spark of the Toddler: Man. It is the symbol of the Macrocosm and the Microcosm; symbol of He on High and of He Below, Symbol of Symbols, for it contains, in its very geometric expression, the holy numbers 3-6-9, the keys to the Worlds having the virtues of the Word.

We have divided these magic numbers into the 'substances' of which they are composed:

3   SPIRIT
33   SPIRIT and ASTRAL
333   SPIRIT, ASTRAL and MATTER

as universal symbol of ascent* and descent, of evolution and involution, and which, by its initiatic splendour, the Triangle completes.

However, for us, this symbol which illuminates the whole of occult tradition with the glowing radiance of its 9

*The French 'l'ascèse' here is properly translated as 'asceticisim' and there is a whole article about it in the *Bulletin* for 9 May 1931. There and here it seems to mean the release that asceticism and renunciation bring, even 'ascension', and here seems better opposed directly to the descent (la chute, or 'fall').

signs (6 figures and the three sides of the Triangle) is also
the symbol of the abiding goodness of this Little Light, 'living close to all and far from all', which one day turned its
compassionate attention to a man who was passing by...

CONCLUSION

THE ROSICRUCIAN KNIGHTS

THE ROSICRUCIAN KNIGHTS

Is this a conclusion? No, only a final account of the Group of Those who, through their communications, advised, enlightened and helped us and allowed us to glimpse, through the thick mists surrounding us, the brightness of the sacred Mountain.

Furthermore, a conclusion would have been dangerous, even 'daring', in view of the tremendous questions raised by this strange Oracle–Method, problems which greatly surpass the aim of these notes. This is why, by way of conclusion, we will merely study here the tendencies of this mysterious Group, its certain links with Agartha which harbours it under the sacred vault of one of its 'Pagodas', and its possible links with 'He Who Waits'.[1]

That this Group is, indeed, part of the initiatic chain of Agartha seems to us to emerge fairly clearly from a group of certain communications; but, as for specifying or localising the spiritual degree they hold in this Centre of the world, in this initiatic omphalos, this surpasses our means of investigation and verification. The symbol of the Trinomial of the Wise Ones (Chiefs of different 'Sacred Mountain' initiatic Groups) being the same for all the Wise Ones, from the Supreme Wise Ones to the Little Lights,[2] how could we be informed graphically on their spiritual hierarchy? Perhaps we could deduce, from the totality of the answers, that the Three Triangles[3] come out 'grouped'

[1]See Appendix, 'The Polaires', page 159.   [2]The numbers 3, 6, 9 written in three triangles.   [3]The 3 triangles with the numbers 3-6-9.

only when the replies evoke, with no doubt whatsoever,
the Supreme Wise Ones; but is that really a symbolic indication of hierarchy? We cannot affirm this. In any case,
what seems to us better to indicate these nuances of Tradition and 'grades' are the various colourings of Light and
their division into 'Light': 'Little Light' and 'Great Light'.
In the various colourings we easily find the Tradition corresponding to the initiatic Group: the Golden Yellow Light
(Buddhist colour *par excellence*), the Green Light (Islamic
colour), sublime Iridescence (indicating the Boreal Tradition, the Boreal dawn being 'iridescent'). We say this
not only based on a symbolic affinity of colours but also,
and above all, because the replies in which we have found
these indications refer precisely to questions of a character that is Buddhist, Islamic, Boreal, etc.

We may not be able to specify, 'localise', the spiritual degree of our Group, but its Latin and Christian (Johannine?)
connections seem sufficiently indicated by the totality of
their direct communications. The superior 'luminosity' of
Christ: 'Light Without Equal', that is to say unequalled,
the evocation of His Word, the Christian philosophy which
obviously emerges from the communications, the Latin
names Julian and Anselm, the mention of Ariosto and,
lastly, the reply concerning the Rosicrucians – all of these
made us believe that we were in communication with the
initiatic tradition of these 'Wise Knights' who, around the
end of the seventeenth century, withdrew, 'taken over by
the Little Lights of the East', to the snowy and invulnerable peaks of the Himalaya. 'Alchemists, Doctors, Cabalists and miracle-workers know what happens in these remote places, applying the Science of numbers to discover

the most hidden of things': the Rosicrucians are described in this way by Heinrich Khunrath in his 'Amphitheatrum Sapientiae',* and our Correspondents, also, seem to have been described in this way through the totality of their communications and by the very essence of the Method. It could be objected that some replies evoked, spontaneously (without any philosophic reason specifically related to the question), the words of the Prophet of the Eternal Black Stone. We found in this, on the contrary, yet another argument in favour of our Rosicrucian hypothesis, given precisely the links of the Rosicrucians with Islamic initiations. Were there not, among their affiliated members, doctors, Arab scientists and Christian Cabalists of purely Jewish origin? (Should we not attribute to their influence the replies evoking the wrath of the fearsome God of Israel?)

If, as we have just explained, we are in communication with a Centre of Rosicrucian Traditions, should we conclude from this that 'He Who Waits'[1] is part of this initiatic Brotherhood? Will this Messenger from Asia come among us under the sign of the Rose, the Cross and the Crescent written in the Tantric Triangle, symbol of a wonderful communion between East and West? Who is this mysterious 'Man'? A communication said 'It will be a Great One who reaches the Supreme Command...'.

He will have the 'Power' and the 'Command', affirm the symbols referring to this Initiate of the highest grade. Great One of the World? Initiate Prince? Uniting in himself the temporal and the spiritual? Renaissance of the Rose and of the Cross? Who can say...? All that we know

---

[1] See page 111

*Actually *Amphitheatrum Sapientiae Aeternae* (Hamburg, 1595)

is that the 'signs' indicate that his coming will be soon and that this great event is in preparation in the Occult.

Every step has been taken so that 'those who know or who see' will no longer be unaware. Soon a second book[1] – or rather a second Message – will perhaps contain precise information about 'He Who Waits'. His mission of Light will be the sign by which will be recognised the tremendous Power with which he will have been invested by mysterious Asia. Will his voice be heard? Will humanity cease its frightening race towards the abyss of gold? Will war, this atrocious spectre which appears, grimacing, in some replies, distance itself from humanity by the will of the Highest? Have not the Voices said 'that this time the atonement will no longer be made by the Son but by blood, and that all humanity will be doubled up under the rods of fire of inexorable Destiny'?

And, in the frantic flight of incredible events which are preparing or developing, it is special to us to see flashing in the occult sky the Sign of Signs, Cabalistic symbol of these Rosicrucians, these 'Wise Knights, Initiated into the Great Wheel', who drew back, about three centuries ago, into mysterious Asia. And it is also special to us to be able to dedicate to them, in all humility, these modest notes.

---

[1]We were not mistaken. 'He Who Waits' is the Supreme Spiritual Chief of the 'Polaires'. They will be under the protection of the Spark of a Wise Knight: a Rosicrucian.

APPENDIX

 *THE POLAIRES*

THE POLAIRES

In June or July 1929 we received, thanks as always to the Oracle of Astral Force, a certain number of communications referring to the formation, or rather the reconstruction, of a Group called the 'POLAIRES'. Given the considerable importance of these communications, we think we should add them to our notes, while profoundly regretting our lack of time and space for comments on them.

This is the first communication, completely unexpected in fact, in which we found information concerning the 'POLAIRES' :

'Form the Group of 'the Polaires' and make it reach across the World – following the indications which will be given to you – on the following theme: 'Light on Spiritualism'.

For one and a half months the operator, as if animated by a new fervour, worked to obtain replies concerning the Group of 'Polaires', some of them were very long (we counted 280 words in one of them) and this vast work is not yet finished.

We have transcribed below the communications received concerning the aims of the 'Polaires'.

The Group of 'Polaires' must have a Statute of 12 articles and 3 Rites. The principal aims of the 'Polaires' are:

- To bring a ray of light where there is only darkness.

- To study, act and bring Truth to where there is only charlatanism.

- To acquire merits and show how they are acquired.

- To reach out across the world by means of a ***Bulletin*** which will be the account of the studies and work of the 'Polaires'.

- To support all wavering Faiths.

- To combat, by every means, the mad fear of death which haunts the human brain. Why tremble if you enter by a better door? Why close your eyes to the Light?

- To combat egotism, the worst of sins, in order to overcome or at least modify it.

- To teach that the bitter struggle of life is necessary and that nothing good, nothing noble, is obtained easily.

- Love for Humanity and absolute Fraternity between the 'Polaires'.

- To protect and help children who are not embraced in love. This mission will be entrusted to the chief of the Women's Group.

- To create – through patient work – Centres in all parts of the world, Centres which in turn will operate to develop and organise the 'Polaires'.

- The Supreme Chief of the 'Polaires' will have the highest spiritual missions, for he must, by his influence, and given the absolute obedience due to him, intervene directly or indirectly to unite men and make them brothers, and to calm down all base human passions.

- Artists – whatever their Art, but those who practise Art with love – will find among the 'Polaires' instructions and advice to avoid the anguish of uncertainty and indecision. In special cases the Three Wise Ones will intervene.

- All 'Polaires' will obtain help and advice from their Chiefs who, in uncertain cases, must ask the Three Wise Ones for Light.

The Polaire will have to acquire merits so as to become 'Polaire 9'.[1]

One of the main aims of the 'Polaires' is to be in contact, through Astral Force X (the Oracle), with an initiatic Group found in the mountains.... Thanks to this Group, the 'Polaires' will have all necessary information on Spiritualism and will also know about life on other planets.

- The 'Polaires' will have to struggle a great deal against impostors and 'bad visionaries', but they will succeed in *reconstructing* what was dispersed by base speculation and by fear of the Light. The Spark of the Wise Knight will protect this work.

- The arithmetic key of Astral Force (the Method) will be handed over to a 'Polaire' when the Wise Knight judges it appropriate...'

The Group of 'Polaires' will thus be under the noble protection of the Spark of a Wise Rosicrucian and, as indicated in an article of the esoteric Statute, its Supreme Spiritual Commander will be 'He Who Waits', the Messenger of *'Asia Mysteriosa'*. The dream of the Visionary, of Saint-Yves d'Alvedre, begins to come true...

Much to our regret, it is impossible for us to also transcribe the 12 articles of the Statute because of their clearly esoteric nature. We will say only that this Statute is essentially non-dogmatic, for the 'Polaire' 'may belong to any religion or have any philosophic opinion, on condition that he is – in his belief or in his conviction – in good faith'. 'Only the way action is taken', say our mysterious Correspondents, 'matters in the elevation of the eternal Spark'.

---

[1]There followed a communication of an esoteric nature, concerning this Polaire grade.

A very important esoteric role is entrusted to the Woman. Indeed, the Initiates remind us in one of their communications that 'what women wish, God wishes'. The spiritual mission entrusted to them: 'protect and help children who are not embraced in love' touches on the sublime. What is more gentle, more touching, than a woman lavishing the infinite treasure of her tenderness on the abandoned child, the suffering child? A marvellous mission, equal in beauty to the mission of Saints.

The articles of this Statute confirm to us that the 'Polaire' movement is, as Dante said, wanted 'there where one can [have] all that one wishes'.* They also confirm that its – REAL – spiritual Chiefs will be Initiates of the highest grade, one could almost say 'transhumanising'. Is not our method of communication with Them – and which must be handed over to a Polaire – irrefutable proof of the 'supranormality'? The esoteric Power of these Chiefs thus constitutes the true Force of this reconstruction. Indeed, the 'Polaires' will not have to obey ordinary men, so much as Initiates who, freed from the mortal grip of instincts and base human passions, will have the power to carry through this formidable task. A ray of Agartha, of *Asia Mysteriosa*, will thus light up this superhuman effort towards Universal Fraternity, towards Light...